Hell and Heaven Revisited

Volume V of My Life

Fred S. "Fritz" Bertsch

2002   2010

Order this book online at www.trafford.com
or email orders@trafford.com

Most Trafford titles are also available at major online book retailers.

Printed in the United States of America.

ISBN: 978-1-4269-4028-6

*Our mission is to efficiently provide the world's finest, most comprehensive book publishing
service, enabling every author to experience success. To find out how to publish your book,
your way, and have it available worldwide, visit us online at www.trafford.com*

Trafford rev. 7/28/2010

www.trafford.com

North America & international
toll-free: 1 888 232 4444 (USA & Canada)
phone: 250 383 6864 ♦ fax: 812 355 4082

Previous autobiographical volumes by Fred Bertsch:

My Paradise; Dad's Hell

Every Day is Navy Day

It's Not School I Hate;
It's the Principal of the Thing

HEAVEN & HELL CHAPTER ORDER

PREFACE

It had been my original intention to write the story of my life in five volumes, covering what appeared to be natural divisions. However, as I reflected on the pain that would be inflicted both upon me and others by writing of the tragic events and circumstances brought about by relating the details of the struggle of and with a beloved but alcoholic daughter and the pain of watching an equally beloved spouse descend into the depths of Alzheimer's disease, I have decided to omit the details of that aspect of my life other than a few references in both Volumes III and V.

AN APPROACHING STORM (1)
A Final Trip

My fourteen year tenure as Principal of Holland High School were coming to an end and my efforts in that position had taken their toll on me. I was exhausted, both mentally and physically, and sought to enter a more placid time of life. My wife, Lory, was completing her twenty year stint as a teacher during the school year after my retirement,

For several years while I was still involved in school administration we had managed to get down to Boynton Beach, Florida, for a week, usually during the school's Christmas vacation, to visit Lory's widowed mother, who owned an apartment there. The tiny one bedroom apartment was just right for her, but when we visited our sleeping accommodation was on the floor of the living room.

As the only surviving Timmer offspring, Lory inherited the little apartment, and it became our Florida alternative home for some time, after which we moved there as our permanent home. In the meantime, our daughter, Martje became engaged in a bitter and lengthy divorce proceeding with her husband Karl. During that time, Lory frequently flew back to Michigan to provide what support she could to our daughter, who complicated the entire situation by becoming a severe alcoholic, a problem that persisted for many years. I joined in a few of those trips, but concluded the neither of us could alter the chain of unpleasant events that was making a number of lives, including ours, miserable.

With the exception of my several visits to Holland, I continued to live in the little apartment in Boynton Beach, relaxing to the degree I could. I fished in the ocean, read copiously, and centered my thoughts on our need for a larger apartment. I visited areas both south and north and soon concluded that we would be most comfortable living somewhere in the area between Stuart on the south and Vero Beach on the north. On one of my visits to Stuart I replied to an advertisement for a three bedroom apartment in a condominium complex named Pierpoint Yacht Club, "For Sale by Owner". My visit and negotiations with the owners and subsequent approval by Lory resulted in our moving to Stuart, where we spent a number of happy years, marred only by our daughter's descent into an alcoholic haze and the usual, although occasional, noisy conduct of our new condominium neighbors.

In one more retirement change we moved to a beautiful and much larger apartment in Hanson's Landing, a part of Miles Grant. Lory had evidenced changes in her mental processes, but we in the family did not consider them at that time to be other than normal human slips. We laughed when she said things like, "The new assistant pastor just graduated from the cemetery last spring," when we knew she meant he had just graduated from theological seminary. She would laugh too; we all misspeak like that from time to time, don't we?

As time went on, she would take a walk and become confused and have to be directed to our condo, even though the buildings were clearly marked. Well, the buildings *are* all alike, or at least similar. We all get confused occasionally and start for the wrong building, don't we?

Another ominous sign arrived after we attended a presentation at the church on the subject of long-term care insurance. We had heard about such coverage and had been involved in conversations dealing with the cost. Most people in our age group seemed to think that the premiums were excessive, and the possibility of collecting on the insurance was minimal, so the conclusion in general was, "We don't need it."

The program at the church was made by a persuasive representative of a major insurance company who accompanied her talk with the slides, films and other materials that often accompany a sales pitch for any product. The question period following her presentation covered a wide range of subjects, including how one would qualify for coverage. The presenter's answer was direct and specific; the candidate for coverage would have to present the results of a complete physical examination plus certification by two physicians that he or she was free of any indications of dementia. She minimized the rigid definitions covering qualification for collecting on the coverage and deftly responded to questions regarding the cost of coverage with responses emphasizing, "Cost for you as an individual will never be less, as the risk to the insurer becomes greater year after year."

As a result of what we had heard at the church Lory and I discussed several times over the next few days whether or not we should have such long term coverage, an idea that seemed reasonable to me in light of the indications that were appearing. However, when we applied for the insurance, although I was accepted for coverage, Lory was not, based on her medical record and an interview with a company-designated physician.

At about this time my close friend, Don Ramage, now retired from the navy as a captain and living in southern California called to let me know that at long last the members of the crew of the *U.S.S. CASE*, the destroyer in which we both had served as junior officers, had decided to hold annual reunions. A preliminary gathering had been held in San Diego, and a second one, also to be in San Diego, was being planned for the near future. I was ecstatic and eager to join my shipmates for three or four days of reminiscences and bull sessions. It would also be an opportunity to visit the familiar sites in San Diego and Coronado that still exerted a considerable pull upon our hearts. I knew that Lory would join enthusiastically in this adventure.

It was not to be. When I broached the subject of attending the reunion, expecting my wife to express immediate support for the idea of spending some time around our old familiar haunts and renewing our friendship with the Ramages, she immediately took a strong stand against the idea. I was stunned, No amount of persuasion could bring her to change her mind. I didn't recognize it at the time, but in retrospect I understand that her change in attitude and her stubborn rejection of the very idea of traveling to our beloved Coronado and the familiar haunts of earlier years was another manifestation of the oncoming storm.

I was determined to attend the reunion with my old shipmates even though Lory was adamantly opposed to our going. In one of the few absolute disagreements of our lives, I flew alone to the three day reunion. Among other activities, I was doused in the swimming pool at the motel serving as the reunion headquarters, carried to the pool by a group of shipmates led by Henry Minor, our notoriously unkempt water tender in *CASE,* who had played the part of Neptune's "baby" during the "crossing the line" ceremony in 1943 during which I became a "shellback." I had a great reunion with my former shipmates.

By the following year, when the reunion was to be held in Norfolk, VA, Lory was reconciled to the fact that I was determined, whenever possible, to attend these reunions and agreed to accompany me. We enjoyed a few extra days in Norfolk, where our son, Buck, now a navy lieutenant commander, was executive officer of *U.S.S. CONTE DE GRASSE,* a newly-commissioned destroyer. He arranged a special tour of the ship for our reunion group and it was apparent that the men of the ship's crew were pleased to show their ship and its armament to these aging destroyer veterans of World War II. There was one more reunion, that Lory was able to attend, this time in Reno, Nevada, after which such travels became impossible.

Some years before all these events, when we first moved to Stuart, Lory had been invited to join the Woman's Club of Stuart. She considered it to be a singular honor to be associated with a group of ladies who considered themselves, it appeared to me, to be among the elite of Stuart. She was proud to be active in the affairs of the club, aspiring in due time to become the president, a position normally achieved only after a member had served in several other executive capacities and most often occupied by a woman who had been a long time resident of the city. Many of the members of the club, and certainly its officers, came from families that had resided in Stuart for several generations. Lory was deeply involved in the process of climbing the ladder of qualifications leading to her goal of the presidency.

After several years of such qualifying steps, while Lory was serving as treasurer of the organization, an occasion arose when an officer of the club phoned to ask me to come and to help her count the small change generated by the sale of refreshments at a monthly meeting. This seemed on the face of it to be a specious request, but its real purpose became clear when the records of the club as well as the bank records showed that Lory could no longer count the quarters, nickels and dimes to obtain a consistent answer. She had to resign her position, and, eventually, her membership. It not only broke her heart; it broke mine as well.

No one, at least not medical professionals, in that period of time, spoke of Alzheimer's disease, other than to remark that it could be diagnosed only after death. We consulted with a psychiatrist, whose name, amusingly enough, was Dr. Dippy. Dr. Dippy referred us to a practicing psychologist, who called in a testing expert, who in turn gave Lory a battery of tests, at the end of which he explained to me in private that Lory had a serious dementia. I must have previously mentioned making a trip with her, for at that time he said, "If you want to take a trip of any length with your wife, you should do it now, and not plan any traveling beyond that." With these ominous words I was left to do whatever planning I could do.

Lory had long expressed a wish to visit her college roommate and matron of honor, Nancy Boynton Prindle, now a widow and living on Cape Cod. We could drive from there for a visit with Lory's brother Jack, who was living in retirement in Maine. Following those visits, as long as we were that far north, we decided to visit our long time friends, Jack and Ruth Laycock, a couple with whom we had had a good time during the Rome convention and other Rotary activities, at their home in St. Stephan, New Brunswick. From there we would drive across Lower Canada to our former home in Michigan for visits with our many friends there. I drove the entire circuitous route, and Lory spent much of the time sleeping. Our hosts, of course, noticed significant behavioral changes in Lory, and remarked about them to me privately.

Her dementia deepened. Lory had been a very good bridge player, and loved the game. Our neighbors, Bruce and May Franklin, with whom we had played bridge a number of times, but with whom we had not played in many months, called one afternoon to invite us to dinner and bridge. I demurred, trying to get them to understand that times had changed, that the skilled bridge player they knew in Lory no longer existed, but had been replaced by someone who looked like her, but who couldn't tell a heart from a spade. Our friends insisted, and found after dealing one hand that I had been in no way exaggerating. They then suggested the board game India, but Lory couldn't move the pieces in accordance with the simple rules of play. It was a frustrating evening for all and a revealing one for our hosts

THE LOTTERY (2)
Winning a Big One

Lory was no longer able to read, although she feigned doing so, holding the newspaper up before her face and moving her head slightly from side to side as she mimicked the actions she had taken before when she was actually reading. Sometimes she would look at the cartoon strips and chuckle a bit. On at least one occasion I observed that she was holding the paper upside down.

All this deceived me for a considerable period of time, although I was learning, albeit too slowly, that the progression of her malady, whatever it was, was unstoppable and irreversible. The doctors we consulted mentioned "dementia" and "cerebral arterial sclerosis" among other potential diagnoses, but never mentioned Alzheimer's disease.

With the introduction of the Florida lottery, Lory had insisted that we buy at least five tickets per week, largely based, initially at least, on the presumption that lottery profits would be used to support improvement in Florida's educational system.

I continued to buy the five lottery tickets each week, and read the winning numbers to her as they appeared in the *Stuart News* on Saturday. Lory would listen intently and express disappointment when, as usual, none of our combinations were winners.

Occasionally, three of the numbers would match one of our tickets, "winning" for us a free ticket. The next time I visited the Publix super market in the Cove Road shopping center, I would pick up the ticket to which we were entitled. It rarely won anything either, but on one occasion it did win another ticket, which, in its turn, won nothing. Once we matched four numbers, and the return was eight dollars.

The picture was clear; we were winning nothing, but somehow it entertained Lory for a few minutes each week, gave me a little diversion from the terrible ordeal that was engulfing our lives, and, relatively speaking, cost very little. At the beginning of the lottery ticket era, I had hung a willow basket next to Lory's desk in the kitchen, and deposited in it all of the worthless tickets after determining each week that they were truly without value.

The ticket basket was almost full as my wife's mental condition continued to deteriorate. It became apparent we would need more physical help than I could provide. Lory could no longer understand winning, losing, lottery, numbers or practically anything. Why I continued to buy another five tickets eacht week is hardly understandable. Why pour more money into the state's coffers? Perhaps I idealized the whole thing by trying to believe that the state would actually allocate the lottery revenues to classroom education as the legislature had promised.

It was Saturday morning, and once again I skimmed the paper's headlines and then turned to page two for the lottery numbers. I compared each of our five tickets with the eight numbers listed for our particular version of the lottery. Suddenly numbers seemed to jump off the paper and match those on one of our tickets. I concluded we once again had a match for four numbers.

This was no big deal; it had happened before and I took it in stride. After all, we had matched four numbers on a previous occasion, and at that time when I presented the ticket at Publix, I was immediately handed the eight dollars such a "win" was accorded. On this occasion I assumed the ticket I held in my hand would be given a similar payout. I stuck it in my wallet for cashing sometime when I was grocery shopping and deposited the other four weekly tickets for the week in the wicker basket to supplement our growing collection of non-winners.

At the time, I was far more concerned with my responsibilities with Lory than I was with collecting a few bucks on a lottery ticket. It was several weeks before I thought again about that ticket in my wallet. Once again in Publix, I had gathered together the few items we needed, pushed my cart toward the check-out counter, took my place in line and reached for my wallet. It was only then that I thought of the ticket that would reap a few dollars when redeemed. As usual, I paid for my little clutch of groceries with a credit card, and then back-tracked to the service counter where the lottery tickets were sold, and where, on rare occasions, small winning tickets were redeemed. Again I stood in line.

Finally, at the head of the line, I presented the ticket to the clerk, and said, "I think I'm due a few bucks for this ticket." She took the ticket and punched the numbers into the machine in front of her. She smiled at me benignly, perhaps thinking what a sap I was for buying lottery tickets.

Suddenly, she let out a shriek, and yelled into a microphone a message that was broadcast throughout the store, "Louie, where are you? I need help!" She then turned back to me and said, now somewhat subdued, "I've never seen one of these before."

My thought was, "One of what?" I only wanted my eight bucks, or so, whatever meager amount that ticket was worth. Louie, the store manager appeared in an instant. What was all the commotion about? Louie and the clerk held a whispered conference. Louie grabbed the ticket and tapped the numbers back into the machine.

He took his time, scratched his head a couple of times, and then reported back to me. "We can't cash that ticket here. We can only cash a ticket with up to five winning numbers....that ticket has seven, and it looks like it's worth several thousand dollars."

He went on to explain that the lottery bureaucracy required me to certify under oath before a notary to a number of things, like name, address, telephone number, social security number, mother's maiden name, place the ticket was purchased, and another dozen or so items I don't remember on a form which he retrieved from under the counter, together with the remark that this was the first such form he had delivered since the lottery was initiated some years before.

Within a few weeks, I received a check for $3,422.17. It wasn't the whole enchilada, but it was close! Had I matched all eight numbers, the win would have been over four million dollars.

When I counted the basketful of "worthless" tickets in the basket, they totaled a purchase price of a little over $3,500.00, so I only lost about eighty bucks to the lottery. Or did I?

Sometimes I am teased about my propensity for saving things of no apparent value, as, for instance, worthless lottery tickets. However, when it came time to file our income tax the next spring, I found that, while lottery and other gambling losses are not normally deductible, losses are allowed to offset winnings up to the extent of those winnings. And thus, essentially, our winnings were income tax free.

AN EVENING OF BRIDGE (3)
"Would You Care for a Cocktail?"

There was at this time a brief escape from my ongoing hell. It was in the middle of a Monday afternoon when the phone rang shortly after I had returned from my daily visit to the nursing home, where I had once again dutifully done the daily difficult, frustrating and even agonizing chore of feeding my wife, who no longer recognized or acknowledged me in any way other than to swallow the gruel or liquefied foods I spooned into her mouth. Who would be calling me? When I picked up the phone, the voice I heard was that of Mary Lou Caldwell, who, with her husband, Pusey, lived in the apartment building diagonally across the swimming pool and club house from ours. I had met the Caldwells at church, and spoken to them in passing on several occasions, but otherwise knew very little about them.

"Pusey and I would like you to join us for bridge on Thursday evening," she announced after the few perfunctory and preliminary inquiries she felt necessary to determine that I knew who she was and also to inquire into the state of my health. At the prospect of socializing over the bridge table I sucked in my breath, perhaps with a bit of a gasp. I had not seen a bridge hand since suffering through a dreadful and humiliating evening with Mae and Bruce Franklin three years before, during which they had finally realized not only that their friend, Lory, could not remember the bid, but couldn't tell a spade from a club, count the cards in her hand or follow suit during play.

Lory had been an excellent bridge player prior to the onset of the Alzheimer demon. It was painful for me to realize that her skillful bridge playing, as well as thousands of other skills, was gone forever. Snapping back to reality, I finally responded, "Mrs. Caldwell, I used to love bridge, but I haven't played a hand in years and don't know if I would be competent to bid or play one now."

"Call me Mary Lou," she responded, "You may be a little rusty, but you never forget how to play bridge, and it doesn't matter at all to us who wins, or whether there are misplays along the way. It simply doesn't matter to us. And beside all that, you've been holed up in that apartment of yours for far too long, and it's time you get out and do some things other than sit and feel sorry for yourself. You're like a hermit. Get off it."

I still wasn't convinced, so, fending for time, I countered, "With whom will I be playing?"

"Dorothy Ridge," she said, referring to the pretty widow lady in Apartment One of the building in which the Caldwells lived, a person who, I was aware, was also a member of Peace Church, and one whom I had observed was a regular in the condominium pool, swimming many laps early in the morning. "You know her from church. She's a great person, a retired nurse." That was more than I had known about Mrs. Ridge prior to that time.

Still dubious, and very unsure of myself, I asked, "What time would we be playing?"

"Eight o'clock," she shot back. "Eight o'clock in our apartment. We'll expect you here at eight o'clock on Thursday, and you'll have a good time." She hung up. I couldn't believe it. I had not stayed up later than eight o'clock for months, and didn't feel that I could possibly stay awake and play bridge for a couple of hours the following Thursday night, or any other night, for that matter. I was at a low point in my life. Everything looked bleak and hopeless. I was in no mood to enjoy a game of bridge. Perhaps I just wanted to be alone and feel sorry for myself. My life was over. All thought of happiness had vanished.

The following day, a notice stuck in my door announced a condominium meeting to be held on Thursday at two o'clock. Although I was not particularly interested in any of the routine items on the agenda, I decided to attend, if only to pass the time. After carrying out my functions at the nursing home and just before the meeting was to begin, I plunked myself down on a chair in the back of the little clubhouse next to the pool and exchanged greetings with several of the men who were sitting there. I observed that the Franklins were in attendance, and that the Caldwells were not. I noted that Mrs. Ridge was seated four or five rows ahead of me.

There was a discussion relative to the placing of the lounge chairs around the pool and an expression of concern about the defecation of dogs around the condominium area together with owners' responsibilities for their pets' activities. The next item was a discourse by the chairman of the social committee, a particularly verbose woman, relative to the best evening or evenings for social gatherings and where and at what time they should be held. All this was fully boring, and my mind was wandering as the droning comments from both the floor and the chair continued. Somehow my attention reverted regularly to the back of Mrs. Ridge's head there a few rows ahead of me, and I wondered how things would go a few hours hence at the bridge table.

Some months before all this, perhaps at Christmas time, our youngest daughter, Mary Jo, had sent eight or ten of those wonderful filets mignon from of the Omaha Steak House mail order catalog and I was fully conscious that two of these epicurean delights were still in my freezer. Although depressed, I never lost my appetite, and now, sitting there as the condominium meeting droned on, and my gaze drifted away from the speaker and toward the back of Mrs. Ridge's head, I started to put the pieces of the situation together in a manner that started to make some possible sense: there was a need to restore my confidence at the bridge table; there was a need for me to become better acquainted with my partner for the evening, and further, a need to determine whether our bidding of bridge hands might be compatible. In my moribund mood it took me a bit of time to organize these thoughts, but I finally decided upon a plan of action. I would invite her to join me in my apartment to explore our joint bridge and then possibly have dinner.

I rose from my chair and moved, almost in a crouch, to a position behind the target and whispered, "Hello. I'm Fritz

Bertsch, and we are supposed to play bridge together this evening." She nodded silently. I said, "I think it would be good  idea if we dealt ourselves a few dummy hands and bid them to see if we could be consistent, informative and compatible in our bidding." She nodded. "Would you like to come up to my apartment for this?" She nodded again. I didn't mention the steaks. "You do know where I live, don't you?" She nodded. I said, "If you leave, I will follow." She didn't nod; she just rose slowly from her chair and departed, with me following a few steps behind, leaving the boring condominium discussion behind us.

We sat on the sofa in my living room and dealt a few dummy hands on the coffee table. It didn't take long to determine that our bidding was compatible and with that, we felt we could hold our own at the bridge table. I then revealed the rest of the plan that had evolved in my head. "Would you like to have dinner with me? I have two beautiful Omaha filets waiting to be grilled, there are potatoes to be baked and I will make a salad that I'm sure you will enjoy."

This time she didn't just nod, but said, "Yes, Fritz, that would be very nice. Thank you." Her response was like music to my ears. I retired to the kitchen, scrubbed the potatoes, put them in the microwave and hurriedly built a salad.

"Do you like blue cheese dressing?" She nodded affirmatively and smiled.

"I usually have a cocktail before dinner, would you like one?"

"A vodka martini on the rocks would suit me just fine."
I fixed the drinks and we retired to the living room. We talked on many topics: the death of her husband; the illness of my wife; her

several activities in the church; our mutual friends, and much more now long forgotten. I fixed a second drink and when it was gone we made our way to the kitchen where I grilled the filets. We ate at leisure, conversed at leisure and the time passed pleasantly. Eventually, I looked at my watch and said, "Oh my, it's five minutes to eight!" and then, perhaps indiscreetly, I said, "I'd better go to the bathroom before we go."

"No!" she said determinedly. "I forgot to tell you that the Caldwells have a guest staying in their apartment, and they asked that we play at my place. We have to be there to greet them at eight. I have bathrooms too, you know. You can go there." We departed in haste.

The apartments in Hanson's Landing are situated in an overall design which places the first and fourth apartment entry doors vis-à-vis each other across the front of the doors of the intervening apartments. The Caldwell's front door thus faced that of Mrs. Ridge's apartment at a distance of forty-five or fifty feet, and they were probably observing our arrival through the peep-hole in their door. My companion switched on the light outside the front door of her apartment as we entered. I headed for the bathroom, and almost immediately the doorbell rang. The Caldwells had arrived.

"Three no trump," I said, to end the bidding of the first hand. I was more confident of the accuracy of this bid than I had been of anything in my life for months. I held a count of fifteen in my own hand! I played the hand and made several overtricks. It was the overture for a great evening of bridge, and at the coda, our score was over four thousand, while the Caldwell's side of the score pad stood at one hundred. We had gone down two tricks on a bid sometime earlier, the only negative in an otherwise perfect evening.

The Caldwells accepted their loss graciously and made their departure. I asked Dottie if she would have dinner with me the next evening, and thereafter we spent time together several times a week, including quiet dinners and church attendance.

HELL ON EARTH (4)
The Situation Worsens

Lory's descent into a hell on earth continued unabated. Although I continued to be a dedicated Rotarian, at least in spirit, regular attendance at the weekly meetings had long since become impossible. On occasion, I would leave my wife alone briefly while I drove hurriedly to the nearby grocery store for a few items of food and other necessities all the while worrying that she would be gone or otherwise in distress when I got back home.

On several occasions she had left the apartment during my brief absences, but neighbors had seen her wandering aimlessly and returned her to our apartment. Bathing, toileting and eating became increasingly difficult problems as time went by. In many ways Lory became an opponent regularly resisting my efforts to aid and care for her. She frequently became violent, slapped me and hit me with her fists as I tried my best to take care of her. My previously loving wife became a fury who regularly abused me with language she would never have used a few years before. Food was thrown about the room, and meals were often brushed from the table onto the floor.

Dressing and toileting became problems. I struggled with all of these and did everything I could to handle the situation, but my efforts were largely in vain and the frustrations approached the unbearable. This situation continued for many months and wore me down. I was exhausted and close to collapse when someone, more knowledgeable than I recognized my situation, and phoned to suggest I call on the Visiting Nurses Association for help. As a result of a phone call, there followed several interviews with the scheduling nurse from the VNA in an effort to determine the amount of help we needed. Based on these investigations this competent woman recommended I hire an aide to come three times per week to assist with Lory's care, and also give me an opportunity to get away, if only briefly.

This situation prevailed for many months, during which time we increased the assignment of the aide in steps from three days per week to four, then five and eventually to seven. The presence of the VNA helper would now give me some freedom of action for a few hours each week. For example, I could attend Rotary for an hour and a half on Wednesday, and do a little grocery shopping after the meeting. I was left with the full responsibility for the patient during the remaining sixteen hours after the helper had left.

The people assigned by VNA were kindly and willing, trained to perform their functions, but largely lacking in communication skills using very limited vocabularies. Most were Haitian and not fluent in English.

Inevitably our situation continued to deteriorate. Even with the help from VNA, I was no longer able to cope with the hour-by-hour care for my wife. Eventually, the VNA nurse recommended that Lory be admitted to the psychiatric ward of a local nursing home. (While things have changed since, at that time a diagnosis of Alzheimer's Disease was not made until after death and while such a postmortem diagnosis was important to the development of medical science, it was of no use to the patient or his family.)

I proceeded to inform our four children of the recommendation of the VNA, and asked for their help in effecting the change when the time came for Lory to move into the nursing home. Telephone consultations revealed that our oldest daughter, Susan, who was Lory's health care surrogate, could not possibly travel to Florida from her Kentucky home at that time. Our second daughter, Martje, living in Michigan was, unfortunately, living in an alcoholic haze. Buck, a commander in the navy, was at sea. This left Mary Jo, our youngest child, now a cardiologist in private practice. She had only recently joined a medical partnership and I was thus reluctant to ask her to join me in placing her mother in her projected new surroundings. There was to be a wait, of course; we had picked the best and, fortunately the most convenient facility in the Stuart area. A patient would have to leave, usually due to death, to provide a vacancy in the dementia unit,

With the concurrence of all members of the family that Lory should be moved to the nursing facility, I completed the application and hoped for a vacancy to occur. Meanwhile, the director of admissions recommended that, if possible, Lory and I make a preliminary visit to her future home as a sort of orientation. During a period of relative calm, I suggested such a visit to Lory, and, to my surprise, she responded favorably. We made a brief tour of the nursing facility, only peering briefly into the locked psychiatric and dementia ward through a window in the door. We returned home, having been assured that the first vacancy would be ours.

The problems at home continued unabated, but at least relief was on the horizon. Within a few weeks I received a call indicating that a vacancy had occurred. I phoned Mary Jo, who, with the approval of her partners, who would share her patient load for a few days, dropped everything on her schedule and flew to our aid, arriving in the late afternoon of the day before Lory was scheduled to be admitted. The arrival of our youngest offspring seemed to have a calming effect on her mother; dinner and the evening passed without untoward event.

With assurances from both me and Mary Jo that "We are going to get you some help," we set off for the nursing home the next morning, and were greeted by the now familiar director of admissions and two other employees, who escorted Lory toward the locked door of the psychiatric wing.

The director of admissions said quietly, "Please leave, and don't return for at least four days. She will need time to become acclimated." It was another heart-breaking and depressing moment. Mary Jo's return flight was not until the next morning, so the afternoon was spent in commiserating. We decided to go to the club for dinner, and it was there that Mary Jo met Dorothy Ridge for the first time. We were joined with a group of friends and had a pleasant time. As we walked home, Mary Jo remarked, "You like Mrs. Ridge, don't' you?" I tried to be noncommittal, but women have insights like that which men do not possess.

For the next two years, with only a few exceptions, I went to the nursing home every day and fed Lory her lunch, frequently having her spitting it out, sometimes at me. On other occasions she would simply sweep her food from her tray to the floor. All of these problems became more intense as time went on. Long after the events of that time I have come to believe that such symptoms are a reaction by the patient to some recognition of the evil forces confronting her or him.

Eventually Lory became comatose and a member of the professional staff would force feed her with a device similar in design to the grease guns formerly used in every garage and car shop in the country. Keeping her relatively clean was a major job in itself, involving hoisting her bodily into a specially designed shower. There were other indignities and she slowly but steadily lost weight. She didn't recognize me, and to me she was anything but the beautiful woman I loved. Despite all, I persisted in my daily visits.

One result of the long agony of suffering resulting from Lory's battle with the devil of Alzheimer's disease was that while she was still at home I spent more and more time in bed, or, at least, in either the bedroom with her and attending to her needs, or on the couch in the living room immediately outside the bedroom door. This phenomenon didn't change when Lory was no longer on the scene. I was like an automaton as I went through my fixed routine and I gradually became more and more isolated from the outside world. The isolation and early retirement for the night continued.

A WELLS TANNERY VISIT (5)
I Meet the Family

Several months later, as the heat and humidity in Florida were increasing toward their summer highs, Dottie announced she was leaving in a few days to go to her "shack" as she characterized it, a house outside of Wells Tannery, itself a dot on the map of Western Pennsylvania lying in a secluded valley surrounded by mountains. It wasn't even an announcement she made; rather, it was a casual comment during the general conversation as we were dining with a group of friends at the Miles Grant Country Club. This development came as a complete surprise to me. She had talked about "The Shack," and some of its history, but I didn't realize how devoted she was to it and how much she enjoyed being there.

Her father had purchased the property on which The Shack stood many years before when Dorothy was a child as a adjunct to the thirty-acre parcel on which stood "The Brick House" his boyhood home. This much I had learned in the few months I had known my new friend.

When I left the dinner group that evening I walked home to my nearby apartment in Hanson's Landing, a section of Miles Grant, feeling a vacancy inside me that refused to retreat. Could this be an inappropriate affection? After all, although my wife was suffering incurably with Alzheimer's disease, she was still alive in the Stuart nursing home and I was there daily attempting, mostly unsuccessfully, to feed her.

Dorothy and I had dinner together one more time before her scheduled departure, and I was brimming with questions, some of which were a bit presumptuous in light of the fact that I had no realistic call upon either her intentions or even her attention. How would she travel to that isolated outpost in Western Pennsylvania, a distance of fifteen hundred miles or so? I knew that she was legally blind and that she occasionally drove a few miles locally under a valid but limited Florida driver's license. She surely would not attempt to drive to Pennsylvania alone. How would she shop for groceries and other supplies? She had mentioned that the nearest shopping center was thirty miles away from her valley house. What if she needed medical care?

As to the first question, she responded that she had arranged with a farmer friend, a neighbor in the valley whom she identified as Ron Black to fly to Florida at her expense and then drive her to the shack. She felt confident she could drive the sixty miles round trip to Bedford for groceries and other supplies. With regard to medical care she breezily announced that except for her eyes she had always been healthy and planned to remain that way.

"I'll be gone until fall," she said and added, to my delight, "Why don't you come for a visit in August? It could be a break in the monotony of your existence here. I'm hosting a family reunion at the shack for my cousins and their families at that time. I'm sure you will enjoy them all."

I tentatively accepted, pending a conference with Lory's doctor as the date for the reunion approached. Lory's condition was steadily worsening as the summer dragged on. In late July she was transferred to Martin Memorial Hospital, and hospice was called, indicating that death was near, but unpredictable. I consulted with the doctor and with the hospice attendants on the question of my attending the Wells Tannery affair. All suggested I go.

Getting to Wells Valley is not easy using any mode of transportation and I found it particularly difficult to schedule travel by air. Driving would take too long since I really could not be absent from home very long under the circumstances. There are only two airports anywhere near the Wells Valley, each thirty miles or more from the shack, and both with only occasional service by small feeder airlines flying equally small airplanes, mostly Beechcraft twin engine planes of a type I had flown occasionally during my naval career. These were planes that had been in service for forty or more years, and now in use by airlines whose future was in about as much doubt as that of the aircraft they flew.

Pittsburgh was the hub from which these small planes flew. Getting to Pittsburgh from West Palm Beach involved a change of planes in Charlotte, North Carolina and waits between planes at each location. I flew into the Martinsburg, Maryland, airport and was driven to the shack by Ron Black, whom I had met at the time he arrived in Stuart to drive Dorothy to her mountain home.

We drove up the interstate to Breezewood and thence east on US30 to the top of Sideling Hill Mountain, at which point we turned left onto Pennsylvania State Road 714. Ron made a cautionary remark, "We drive down this mountain in second gear. We can control the vehicle better that way. Some of it's pretty steep and the turns are pretty tight." Both statement were true. Shortly we were at the bottom of the mountain. I later learned that this was often called "Kirk's Bottom", a reference to Mrs. Ridge's grandfather.

I really didn't know what to expect as we drove along next to a wire fence on rutted lane and thence across a plank bridge onto a meadow bounded by two creeks. The shack, nestled against the side of a wooded hill overlooked both meadow and the creeks.

The meadow was filled with people, young and old. Some were wielding mallets and driving croquet balls through the wire wickets on an improvised court laid out on the rather bumpy surface of the area. Boys were flinging unpowered model airplanes into the air, while girls were blowing soap bubbles that floated over the whole scene. A couple of adults were playing catch with a soft ball, and all seemed to be having a good time.

My introduction was brief and I was confronted with the need to attempt to remember the names of what seemed like a hundred cousins, nieces, nephews and assorted spouses. It wasn't long before it was time to have a picnic dinner, and the whole serving table was set up inside the shack because as twilight fell the air was filled with a combination of mosquitoes and lightning bugs.

We all fell into a jagged line and loaded our trays with the traditional picnic foods of summer. I found myself wondering, "Where will all these people sleep? Where would I sleep?" I was tired from all my travels and the natural pressure I felt in meeting many people new to me. I was not eager to sleep out under the stars with what seemed like all the mosquitoes and lightening bugs in the world as my hosts.

I was only slightly relieved when one of the cousins announced, "We've made reservations for a couple of nights at the Ramada in Breezewood, so we'll see you all bright and early in the morning for breakfast." I recognized the name Breezewood, as Ron and I had passed through it on our way to the shack from the Martinsburg airport. Another couple of cousins, Fred and Ginna Modavis announced that they were also headed for the Ramada.

"But don't plan on us for breakfast. Fred has to eat within fifteen minutes after he gets up, or things don't go right for the rest of the day." That still left a sizable group of people with no place to sleep as far as I could tell, but I was soon proven wrong. The remodeling that had been done many years before included the addition of a great room extending from the original living room out toward the second of the creeks and it included a beautiful stone fireplace.

"All you kiddoes get ready for bed," was the next announcement, and eventually, amidst much objecting, whimpering and praying all juveniles were tucked into sleeping bags that had been carried to the scene by the visitors having children and eventually it was quiet in the great room. One set of parents announced they were tired and ready for bed. They were assigned to a pair of the four davenports in the great room.

This left four of us, Mrs. Ridge, her married cousins, Les and Elaine Armstrong and me. The Armstrongs, long favorite cousins, appeared to know exactly where they were to sleep and they headed for the guest bedroom that had been added to the second story of the building during one of the many times the house had been remodeled. Dorothy led me to a room off the kitchen, one of the other additions to the tiny original house. "You get to sleep here Fritz," and then, much to my relief, she added, "I'll make up the sleeper couch for you."

The only bedroom in the original house was upstairs over the living room, and that was taken by our hostess. With all of these sleeping assignments having been made, as I learned later, there were still two unoccupied sofas in the great room and an iron springless cot in the hallway at the head of the narrow stairway standing between the two bedrooms. In the **final analysis there were sleeping places left unoccupied.**

The culminating activity of the reunion of cousins was a dinner Sunday evening at the Days Inn atop Town Hill

Mountain. It was a squeeze, but we managed to fit ourselves into a table set between the kitchen and the bar. The next morning, all had departed for home except for Dottie's cousins, Les and Elaine, who, I learned, had made a practice for years of staying over for a day or two after the reunion.

We passed a pleasant morning, talking about the reunion, events of the community to the extent Mrs. Ridge knew of them and then the national scene. Elaine's passion was bridge and so a part of the afternoon was spent at that recreation. I was happy that earlier I had had a refresher course during our evening with the Caldwells.

Late that evening we received a phone call from Martje saying that Lory had died. In a flurry of phone calls we strived successfully to arrange my expeditious return to Stuart .

LORY'S DEATH (6)
The End of an Era

A call from our daughter Martje, who had flown to Florida upon receiving the news that Lory was being transferred to hospice care, announced Lory's death. It was a shock, even though I had anticipated she would die in the near future, but after I had returned to Stuart, The call prompted immediate action to get me back to Stuart as expeditiously as possible. I had flown into Pittsburgh on U. S. Air on my trip to Pennsylvania, and then to Martinsburg, Pennsylvania by small plane en route to the shack. A return by that circuitous route in reverse would be anything but expeditious. Les offered to drive me wherever I had to go.

We called Continental Airlines and they had a flight departing Harrisburg at five the next morning for Baltimore-Washington International. We leaped at that opportunity to get to an airport through which a major airline operated. After booking that flight we requested routing to West Palm Beach. In just a few minutes the agent had booked my travel from Harrisburg to BWI, thence the short hop to Washington International (later Reagan International) at which point I would board a U. S. Air flight to Charlotte, North Carolina for a change of planes and thence onward to West Palm Beach. In each case the schedule allowed for only a brief time between flights. In retrospect, such a schedule would not be attainable with the restrictions placed on air travel following the attacks on the World Trade Center and The Pentagon. If any of the flights were to be late by even a few minutes, I would have been stranded, but in the event, all went well.

I called Martje at our apartment and told her of the proposed schedule and the danger that I might be delayed. She informed me that Buck was in the air en route to West Palm and that he could wait for us until we got there, if we did. She would call U.S. Air and have him paged. Thank God she was sober. I think her mother's death kept her that way, at least for the time being.

I threw my few things into my bag, and we were off for Harrisburg. Fortunately, Les made a habit of gassing his car immediately after the end of a trip over any significant number of miles, so his tank was full. In contrast with the rest of my schedule, I had plenty of time before the departure from Harrisburg, and fortunately the itinerary worked to perfection. Son Buck was waiting for me at West Palm Beach.

The next few days are a blur in my memory. We advised all of the relatives by telephone. In a short time all of our children arrived together with some of our grandchildren and we arranged accommodations for them. Lory's brother, Jack, sent a telegram announcing he would not be able to attend the funeral. There was no explanation in his message of why he was not coming to his sister's funeral.

I wrote an obituary for the Stuart, Holland and Muskegon newspapers, inadvertently and unfortunately omitting Jack's name. He would never forgive me for this omission, even though I apologized profusely for the all-too-human error. Although we had made a considerable effort to visit him on our farewell trip three years before, when we knew that Lory would not be able to travel after that, Jack never bothered to visit his sister in Florida before or after her death. Closure came only a few years later, when his wife called to inform me of his death.

Our minister at Peace Presbyterian Church, Reverend Jim Bailey arrived shortly after he knew of the long anticipated death and a funeral service was planned. I emphasized our family's desire for an informal service to include family participation and Jim was happy to conform to our wishes. His eulogy was brief and appropriate. I rose and managed to get through a short but heart-felt monologue of love and devotion with heavy emphasis on the happy times of our lives.

Particularly moving were presentations by Skipper and Gail Shipley, the two children of our oldest daughter, Susan.

Grandmother Lory, with some assistance from me had cared for Skipper during one year-long absence of their mother while she was on military duty that precluded her caring for him, and later we cared for both children during another military absence.

As we requested during the planning for the funeral, Janet Bailey, the minister's wife, played show tunes from the forties and fifties during the less formal parts of the funeral. Those in attendance agreed that it was a beautiful and appropriate service. Our son would attend to the details of delivering her funeral remains after cremation to Arlington National Cemetery, where after my death I will join her in a designated crypt.

In mid afternoon we gathered for a light lunch at the Miles Grant Country Club and an era had come to an end.

GETTYSBURG (7)
A Proposal

Dottie was enjoying the summer in Wells Tannery, while I was miserable and lonely in Stuart following Lory's death. I talked to Dottie several times on the phone and expressed my feelings about the death of my wife, but also my increasing interest in her, now at least with some legitimacy. Dottie was not so sure, but she finally agreed to allow me to visit her again at the shack as a diversion from my misery. It was by then early October, and it would not be long before the snowbirds started returning to Florida, she among them.

I did not at that time understand the dilemma in which my prospective hostess found herself. I just thought she was wondering what to do to entertain this invader, but she was also concerned about the neighbors. Wells Tannery is a very small, well-knit community in which, generally speaking, everyone knows what everyone does in the community, and if there is any deviation from the norm someone is bound to detect it and insure that all others in the valley also know about it. There were some well known cases where everyone in town heard about some individual's alleged misbehavior except for the alleged miscreant himself. The widow Ridge did not want to run any risk of besmirching her reputation via some misunderstood misstep.

Although I was but one driver, I was the owner of two flaming red Cadillacs repainted over more somber colors and I chose the newer of the two for my travel to Southwestern Pennsylvania. I rose well before dawn on a Friday morning, fixed myself a bit of breakfast and a couple of sandwiches for a day long drive and hit the road; I-95 to the beltway around Washington D. C., I-70 to Breezewood, US-30 exactly five miles to the top of Sideling Hill Mountain and then a turn to the left down the mountain on State Road 915 exactly five miles to the lane leading to the shack at Kirk's Bottom, two miles from the village of Wells Tannery. It had been a drive of almost a thousand miles.

Prior to my departure from Stuart, I had received instructions from myhostess on how to drive down the mountain: "After you turn onto 915 there is a short rise in the road, but from that point on, it's down the mountain through steep grades and very sharp turns, so shift into second gear to slow your descent and save your brakes. Don't let your speed get over thirty miles an hour. You'll save on both the brakes and your nerves if you do," she told me.

She had further instructions, "At the bottom of the mountain there is a fairly sharp curve with a barn to your left. That's my barn, so let the car slow down. Shortly after you straighten out there is a lane that leads to the shack. If you see a wire fence to your left, or the brick house, you've gone too far. You remember the bridge over the creek from your last visit. Park anywhere."

It was already getting dark wjen I crossed the bridge. My hostess had spotted me as I passed the barn and came to the porch to greet me with a kiss on the cheek for which I was thankful. I wanted to use the bathroom and was reminded that the facilities were divided between "a girl's room" which contained a stool, a wash basin and a bath tub, while the "boy's room" contained a stool, a wash basin and a shower stall. I was tired and hungry following my long drive, so after a simple meal I was directed to the now familiar "old living room" where I had bedded down on my previous visit. and slept profoundly until dawn.

Dottie appeared from upstairs, disappeared briefly to the girl's room and then started to prepare breakfast. "After breakfast, pull yourself together, and gather up whatever you need for the day. You told me once you were a history buff, so we're going to Gettysburg. There's plenty of history there." This was a defense against the village gossipers, but I didn't know it at the time. I was happy for the opportunity to spend some time on "hallowed ground."

"How far is it to Gettysburg?" I inquired.

She replied, "A little less than an hour. We can visit a few of the sites, have lunch and be back here by dusk. You'll enjoy it." I was sure I would.

We started out promptly and drove that steep twisting road up to the top of the mountain at route thirty, where we turned left, going east. Again we were involved with steep grades and radical curves, but on a somewhat better road than 915. I was impressed by the several runaway truck ramps running up to the right on the mountain as the road descended rapidly.
En route we passed this two hundred year old log house still used as a dwelling. In other areas we encountered houses built of field stone.

Dottie pointed out an antique shop at Harrisonville and we then took the by-pass around McConnellsburg, the county seat of Fulton County. En route to Chambersburg we passed through several towns, one of which sported houses built a century or so ago facing directly on the highway with just a few feet between them and the automobile traffic. Finally we were at Gettysburg.

We spent the rest of the morning exploring a portion of the battle ground, recognizing that viewing every important monument and view would take a week or more. It was surprising to me how much of the field of action covered during the three day battle was accessible by automobile. We drove to Little Round Top and found the monument marking where the Michigan division of volunteers had held their ground to the last man. It was then on to the high water mark of the Confederacy at the wheat field.

After a late lunch I insisted that we visit the cemetery and then the Gettysburg Panorama, a privately owned presentation of the three day battle. We were late for a performance and settled for tickets to the next showing. In the interim we viewed the extensive collection of battle artifacts on the lower level including a large number of the actual rifles and smooth bore weapons carried by the opposing armies, handfuls of the lead bullets recovered over the years, and assorted pieces of equipment, artifacts and soldiers' personal gear.

It was dusk when we left the Panorama and I remarked that I didn't relish the thought of returning to the Tannery and driving those final treacherous roads in the intense darkness of the surrounding forest. "Why don't we just go to the Ramada, book a couple of rooms and have a leisurely dinner? We can drive home in the morning when we're refreshed. I will feel much better about it that way." I gave no thought to the fact we were in a popular and historic town saturated with visitors on a weekend night.

We stopped at the Ramada and asked for one non-smoking single room and one where smoking was permitted, as I was still smoking cigars in those days. The kindly lady behind the desk said, "With the exception of one non-smoking room with a single king-size bed, we are booked for the weekend." I was stunned.

She added, "I'll call around to the other accommodations in the area, but in the meantime I'll hold this room for you in case you want to take it."

She proceeded with her calls and as she was doing so another older couple arrived and announced their need for a room. The clerk gave them the same response she had given us, but added that she was holding the one remaining room for us. If we didn't want it they were next in line. Her phone calls around the area yielded no results. I said, "We'll take it," and visualized an uncomfortable night trying to sleep in the car in the motel parking lot while my hostess was sleeping dreamlessly in the vast expanse of that kingly bed.

We went to the room. I was tired and the bed looked bigger, softer, sweeter and more appealing than any bed I had ever seen. I kept my cool, but my mind was operating at full capacity. I concluded I could sleep on the floor or in the bath tub. Would the motel provide extra linens? I didn't know. "There is a small magazine boutique off the lobby," I offered, "I'll go down and see if I can buy a couple of toothbrushes."

I returned with the toothbrushes and even a small tube of tooth paste. I also had a fully formed suggestion, "I am an officer and a gentleman, and under no circumstances do I intend to attack or rape you. If we ever have sex in the future it will be at our joint volition and not due to any forceful act of mine. I see no sense in your occupying this huge bed by yourself while I sleep on the floor. If you agree, I will leave and give you complete privacy as you undress tonight and dress in the morning. I'll use the men's room off the lobby and put one of these numerous pillows between us as we sleep."

It was quite a compelling speech, I thought. To my great relief she smiled and nodded. "All right," she said, "I trust you." We went to dinner and talked of other things. Per our agreement I stayed in the lobby while she went to the room to prepare herself for bed.

The arrangement worked well and I slept soundly on my one third of the bed while Dottie, a rather small person, occupied the other two thirds. The room was drenched in sunlight when I woke up. It was after seven. I pulled on my clothes, grabbed my toothbrush and headed for the lobby. My companion continued her regular breathing punctuated with a gentle purr.

After performing my limited toileting, I bought a Sunday paper and a cigar at the lobby news stand, poured myself a cup of coffee and settled down for what was bound to be a lengthy wait. Eventually I decided she had had enough time, so I called from the lobby phone, and on inquiry found she was ready for breakfast. Over our meal we laid a few plans, one of which was to attend the second service at what had come to be known as Eisenhower Presbyterian Church although this was not its official name. We hoped to see the former president and his wife, Mamie, but we were informed early that they attended an earlier service in order for Ike make it to the golf course for an eighteen hole round.

We arrived considerably before the scheduled time of the next service and took seats in a pew toward the front of the church an accommodation to Dottie's limited eyesight. We seated ourselves in a pew just ahead of a parishioner, who, upon our arrival inched his way to a position behind Dottie and slightly away from the side where I was sitting.

I was somewhat displeased when he leaned forward and began a lengthy dissertation on the history of the church, its participation in the underground railway, its role in the Civil War in general and its efforts on behalf of the freed slaves. Partially I was displeased because he whispered all of this history into Dottie's ear, and I was left hearing only a small part of it.

We had a nice lunch at a Gettysburg restaurant and then drove back to the shack, where we fixed a light supper and then sat on the screened porch and talked for hours. We wound up the day by proposing to each other. It had been a wonderful two day adventure.

<u>COURTING(8)</u>
Another Set of Life's Dilemmas

Out of the blue one afternoon, Susan, the oldest of our daughters called from Las Vegas a destination she took about once a year from her home in Kentucky to satisfy an urge to be under the bright lights on the gambling scene there. Her call was actually an invitation, an opportunity for me to get away from the grinding life that had worn me down. "I have all these complementary privileges from previous gambling junkets. So I can provide you with a room, your meals and a few other things if you cared to join me for a few days."

The offer intrigued me, and it would give me an opportunity to shed the immediacy of what I saw as my duties in Stuart, but I was reluctant to accept Susan's offer. "Gee, Sue I'd love to get away from here, but I wouldn't feel right leaving right now," stalling for time while I thought about her offer. We talked about other things for a few minutes, but then I came back with a revelation for Sue that I was truly interested in this widowed neighbor lady named Dorothy Ridge.

"Bring her along," said Sue, always ready to advance an already developing social situation, "I can comp you both, and it'll only cost you the plane fare." This just about did it. I am not an addicted gambler, but I do like tossing those "galloping dominoes" on occasion, sometimes with considerable success. I reminded myself that my luck one night in Iwakuni, Japan had enabled us to build a house in Coronado, California. "I'll have to talk to Dottie before I make a decision," I concluded, "I'll get back to you forthwith."

I'm not sure I was entirely candid with Dottie about the details of this proposed visit to "Sin City", but I did convince her that it would be fun, if not exactly the opportunity of a lifetime.

Sue called again to firm up a few details and revealed that she would be accompanied by a "friend", a woman who was the night supervisor or foreman over the several other employees in husband Greg's plastic molding operation that was producing as a sub contractor thousands of various molded products used by many manufacturers. It was a twenty four hour per day continuous operation, or, as a they say "twenty four, seven." Greg volunteered to cover both day and night shifts to allow his employee to accompany Sue.

The friend joining her was the woman night supervisor or foreman over the several other employees in husband Greg's plastic molding operation producing thousands of various products used by many manufacturers. It was a twenty four hour per day operation, and Greg had volunteered to cover both the day and night shifts for a few days to allow his employee to accompany Sue on a gambling junket to Las Vegas for a couple of days of gambling. It was a nice gesture, he thought.

Dottie and I arrived a day after Sue, having flown the "red eye" all night. After a cab ride to the hotel, we found her in the hotel casino playing the dollar slots with gusto. She broke off her efforts at pushing silver dollars into her favorite mid-casino slot machine long enough to greet us and accompany us to the room, for which she had already procured the keys. As we went, she explained that the room was a promotion award from the hotel based on her gambling on previous visits and that she had originally reserved it for her employee-guest, but under the circumstance would have her guest join her in her room, which was furnished with twin beds. Sue also handed us a sheaf of comps for meals and suggested that we go to the grill for breakfast.

We were astonished when we entered the room. It was the hotel's lavish honeymoon suite sporting a mammoth super king-sized bed with a canopy of lace curtains hung from the ceiling over the bed matching the curtains at the window overlooking The Strip. There also were heavy blackout drapes to block out the glare and bedlam on the street below. There were two baths with adjoining dressing rooms. Neither of us had enjoyed a room as extravagant as this before.

After a bit of bathroom time, we headed off to the grill on the mezzanine for a breakfast. The meal on the plane had been adequate, but was "airplane food" and left us ready for a real meal. The grill menu offered what seemed like a hundred options, but we were content with our favorites; Dottie with a vegetable omelet and I with steak and eggs, all accompanied with juice, my coffee and Dottie's herbal tea.

Following this ample breakfast, we collapsed on the bed for a few hours before joining Sue in the casino, where she was once again busily shoving silver dollars into her favorite one-armed bandit. For me, who had never played a slot machine equipped to take anything richer than quarters, it was a bit of a shock to watch Sue pushing all that money into oblivion. When I commented on the rate at which her silver dollars were disappearing, she said, "Don't worry, Dad. I won a thousand dollar jack pot while you were at breakfast or sleeping. Now I'm just trying to hit the grand jackpot that is guaranteed to contain at least fifty thousand dollars." Once again I was astonished; I would have walked away with the thousand, but here was Sue pushing it all back into the machine until she had lost it all, or at least that is what I expected.

We strolled over to the only operating craps table where six or eight stalwarts were watching the dice, or galloping dominoes bounce off the back board to accompanying cheers or moans depending on the result of the roll. It was a two dollar table and I decided I'd either drop a few bucks or pick up a few with small bets on the come line. I was surviving on my ten dollar take out, winning a few and losing a few, talking to the players and listening to the jargon of the dealers when it happened..

There was a sudden roar of voices from the slot area, followed by a bedlam of horns, bells, whistles and other assorted noise makers. Susan had hit the ten thousand dollar jackpot and was hanging onto the machine while waiting for verification of her win and the money, which came in the form of a cashier's check. The casino photographer was on the scene before the check arrived, and when it did Sue and her check were photographed in as many different poses as the photographer could think of, with the big winner smiling happily throughout the session. Several of the pictures were included in subsequent issues of the casino's newsletters, distributed widely to players and guests, and used for other publicity purposes.

After this victory, Susan mailed the big check to herself via registered mail and then started playing the nickel and quarter machines. We concluded she wasn't so dumb after all. In a celebration gesture, the big winner invited us to join her in the most elegant of the hotel's dining rooms for a dinner at which the piece de resistance was a crown roast of lamb. We had several drinks, enjoyed the lamb and finally when the check arrived Sue broke out her complimentary coupons and presented them as payment. "Sorry madam," said the server, "But these comps are valid for food only at dining rooms C and D. We will accept cash, a valid credit card or we can charge the bill to your room."

Sue winced, but signed the check. She could well afford to do so, but her nature forbade her to accept this treatment without a fight. When we next saw her she proudly displayed the casino's bank check to offset the fancy dinner bill.

MARRIAGE (9)
A Premarital Tangle

One of the immediate questions was where we should live after our wedding. We agreed that it would not be appropriate to occupy either of our apartments with all the emotional baggage of memories we each carried. It would be better, we thought for us to buy a place that would be ours rather than "mine" or "hers." We consulted with Chick Hahn, a friend of Dottie's, a realtor who was particularly active in the sale of Miles Grant properties.

Among the properties presented to us as possibilities was a three bedroom, two bath house with a lanai overlooking a creek running through a small forest preserve within a section of Miles Grant named Hanson's Circle. The back yard included a Honey Dew orange tree and a pink Indian River type pink grapefruit tree, both loaded with fruit. A small lime tree could provide the owners with an unlimited supply of limeade and twists for cocktails. It was perfect for our needs and we quickly arranged to buy it.

During the planning of our wedding, we requested three different forms of music, the Wedding March, the Navy Hymn and Dottie's favorite, *Amazing Grace.* Janet Bailey, the minister's wife suggested, since we had lived long lives, we might want to include some of the contemporary music we had enjoyed over our lifetimes and we readily agreed. During the actual ceremony she would play a subdued *Hawaiian Wedding Song* on the organ and later as the final one of the series she would play *I Want to Go Back to My Little Grass Shack in Kaulakahu Hawaii,* a recognition that we planned a belated honeymoon trip to the islands. A number of our guests later remarked favorably about our decision to include popular music.

Following Lory's death, thanks to the earlier estate work of our attorney, Greg Keane, it appeared to us there were only a few details to monitor, as the interests of our children and grandchildren were already carefully defined and protected, we felt. A few months sped by, during which Buck received orders to command a a group of Guam based ships that were combat loaded for support of a marine brigade in case of an emergency in the Far East.

In preparation for this command, Buck was to spend a few days in Jacksonville aboard a similar ship preparing for deployment elsewhere. I planned to drive there from Stuart and spend some time with my son before he left for Guam by air. In the course of the visit, I explained to him the relationship that had been developing between Dorothy Ridge and me, including the possibility, or even the probability that we would be married sometime in the future. His response at that time was that he hoped we would hold off on any marriage plans we might make would be put on hold until after his return from his new assignment. His unaccompanied tour was scheduled for one year. I offered the comment that we both were in our upper seventies, and that the time Dottie and I would have together would probably be brief. Our conversation turned to other subjects and we spoke no further of the matter during my short visit.

Dottie returned from her summer in Wells Tannery, and we began active planning for an early marriage. By that time Buck had left by air to join his new command in Guam. I really felt that our wishes should prevail and be respected by all members of our extended families. In that, as with so many things in life, we discovered later we were wrong.

Early on, we met with Reverend Jim Bailey, our minister, who had, of course, taken note of our regular church attendance in company. After listening to our rationale, and our desire to be married sooner rather than later, he counseled us to proceed. We set a date of January 17, 1998, reserved the church and planned for a luncheon reception at Miles Grant Country Club. We invited Dottie's cousin, Elaine, to be her matron of honor and my life-long friend Bill Jesiek to be my best man.

We invited something over a hundred guests for the wedding and a luncheon to follow, including Dottie's children and grandchildren, her cousins and their families, my children and grandchildren, my longtime friends Bill and Peggy James and an entourage of our mutual friends mostly living in Miles Grant. Unfortunately, Dottie's daughter Kathleen and her husband Jim felt they could not attend due to the distance from their home in the state of Washington.

We planned with Reverend Bailey a rehearsal at the church for the ceremony a couple of days in advance of the actual marriage and also planned to entertain the wedding party at a small dinner at Miles Grant following this preview

We arranged accommodations for invited family members, our wedding party, and several dear friends from out of town who would be arriving early and invited all to join us for a rice and curry dinner at our new home on the evening before the wedding.

As we were mature adults in our late seventies, having made our own life decisions over many years, it never occurred to us that we needed the approval or permission of anyone else in this case. We were wrong.

We were aware that our impending marriage would have some legal ramifications for both of our estates, and we met in a timely way with my attorney, Greg Keane, who agreed to serve as Dottie's attorney as well mine, at least for the most part. At this meeting he agreed to prepare a revision to my will providing for Dottie in case of my untimely death, together with a few other revisions and, also to draw a will for Dottie in accordance with her wishes.

At Attorney Keane's insistence, we agreed to sign a pre-nuptial agreement covering everything he could think of to occupy a dozen or more legal pages. This document was to be ready several days before the wedding and we scheduled an appointment with Mr. Keane to sign it and the other legal documents he had prepared, including our living wills, appointments of health care surrogates, and others.

As I signed all of the documents prepared for me, they were passed along to Mr. Keane and two other witnesses, his secretaries. It was then Dottie's turn to go through the same procedure, except that when it got to the prenuptial agreement, in a move unexpected by us, the attorney announced that he could not counsel Dottie in this matter, as that would involve a possible conflict of interests. With that, he recused himself, and said he would contact another attorney to review the agreement with Dottie. It was now late in the afternoon three days before the scheduled wedding. After a few phone calls, Greg located an attorney who agreed to review the document with Dottie, and made an appointment for her to meet him in mid morning the next day, two days before the wedding.

Dottie and I left the house for our scheduled meeting with the new attorney. At his office, after a short wait, he greeted us and waved toward his private office. His left hand wave was for Dottie, while his right hand, practically shoved in my face, indicated I was to remain outside. They would review the document in private, and I was left cooling my heels outside for a couple of hours while he explained to Dottie the meaning of every sentence in every paragraph of the agreement, which meanings Dottie felt she already knew. When they reappeared, the attorney indicated that the prenuptial agreement, as slightly revised by him, would be ready the next day.

We went off to the rehearsal, received all of our instructions from our friendly pastor, gave custody of the rings to Bill and Elaine and went off to the small post rehearsal dinner we had planned to have at the club, feeling that things were on track and all would go smoothly from that point onward. Little did we know. I spent the next morning preparing the chicken curry, the associated condiments and side dishes we planned to serve informally to our guests that afternoon and early evening as they arrived. It seemed to us that our preparations were complete, so when the attorney's office called and said the prenuptial agreement was ready for Dottie to sign she felt free to leave for a short time, sign the document and return.

Among the guests who had already appeared were Martje, my alcoholic daughter, and her new-found husband, Calvin, also an alcoholic, who appeared looking like a societal derelict from a hobo camp. That day he was wearing a torn collarless shirt, ragged cutoff jeans shorts, dirty floppy sandals and a three-day growth of beard. In addition, he was about three-months overdue for a haircut. It was he who volunteered to drive Dottie to pick up her document.

On arrival at the attorney's office, the secretary, holding the agreement, demanded payment of a considerable sum of money before releasing it. Dottie, who was not carrying her purse said, as is usual under such circumstances, "Bill me. You have my address."

The secretary, obviously under instructions from her boss, said, in an extremely loud voice, "Get out! Get out, or I will call the police." No entreaty would satisfy the secretary, so the two left to come home and confer with me.

I called Greg Keane to protest. He called the offending attorney and Dottie and I, making another ten mile trip, retrieved the agreement. The attorney did not appear, but the bill, of course did. We paid it several weeks after the wedding.

Meanwhile, the wedding participants and our family members were arriving at our new dwelling, where the tile floor in the lanai had been torn up for installation of new tile to replace the old, some of which were broken and all of which were not to our taste. The tile layer had promised the new floor would be completed well before any of our scheduled wedding activities but he later called to announce delivery had been delayed and he apologized profusely, but this left us a mess on an unusable lanai.

Fortunately, among the first to arrive were my daughter Susan Bobek and daughter-in-law Cindy Bertsch, who proceeded to insure that the assembling group was served a platter of warm curry over rice, together with the appropriate condiments and side dishes. On our return to the gathering, our impression was that all attendees were mixing well and, in general having a good time. As the gathering dispersed, we retained that impression and departed for our respective apartments for our last night apart.

The morning of the wedding was a blur to me, although I did note it was a beautiful January day in Florida, with just a few puffy clouds moving across the otherwise cloudless sky.

With a couple of notable exceptions, all of the invited guests appeared, along with a smattering of other uninvited folks, most of whom we recognized but among the uninvited were a few strangers all of whom took occupancy in the rear pews of the church. I have often wondered whether these folks attended weddings of people they didn't know as an inexpensive recreational activity.

The ceremony was traditional and all went smoothly with Bill Jesiek and Elaine Armstrong at our sides performing their functions with grace and equanimity. The interlude of popular music played on the organ by the minister's wife, Janet was well received by our guests, and several remarked on how appropriate it was.

It was planned the guests would depart from the receiving line and reassemble at the country club for the luncheon. We prepared in advance a little set of directions to the club, a simple matter since the next property to the church on Cove Road was Miles Grant and the road ended at the Intracoastal Waterway, which was also the eastern boundary of Miles Grant. The clubhouse of the Miles Grant Country Club is most conveniently arrived at by taking the third entry after the church and then turning left through the parking area to the main entrance. Unfortunately in the directions I had written they said enter the second exit from the road rather than the third. With one exception, all of our guests recognized the error and had no difficulty in finding the club.

The exception was Dottie's cousin Robert Schrieber and his wife, Elsie who made the turn at the second entrance and then the second left turn onto the back side of Miles Grant Road past the eighth and tenth holes of the golf course. Had they continued on this circuitous route, they would have arrived at the club house without difficulty, but they chose to wander around through the residential parts of Miles Grant. We at the luncheon noted that they had not arrived, but knew nothing of their adventures.

The Baileys had told us they had a short errand to complete before coming to the reception luncheon and we anticipated their late arrival. Dottie and I seated ourselves at separate tables and invited all who wished to imbibe to order a glass of wine or a cocktail. The servers were in the process of serving the drinks when the Schreibers entered the dining room following immediately after the Baileys who quietly seated themselves at the places we had reserved for them.

Not so the Schriebers. Robert, one of Dottie's cousins, a rather demure and patient individual, seated himself quietly, but his wife, Elsie, would have none of that. She insisted in a loud voice that the directions to the club were totally wrong and that someone should be held accountable for the grave error. I was the one in error and had prayed forgiveness for any inconvenience I might have caused but I was not prepared for what happened next. Elsie gave me a tongue lashing that has remained in my memory as a significant event on my wedding day, although she used no profanity it was a verbal buggy whip that lasted for several minutes. Many at the gathering laughed as they sipped their drinks and eventually the one person tumult subsided. It had simply added some further color to our happy day.

While making our plans for post nuptial activities, we took into consideration the distances people would travel and the fact that we were uniting two families, the members of which had had little or no opportunity to know each other. We wanted to accommodate the needs and desires of all concerned to the best of our abilities; it was our party and we decided, among other arrangements, to extend ourselves and serve a full course dinner to all invited guests.

Both before and after we had eaten, Dottie and I passed among the guests and it appeared to us that all present had had a good time. Even Elsie had calmed down by the time the meal had ended. We heard no dissent from the members of our families. There was no indication to us of disapproval of our marriage.

Because those who had traveled long distances to attend were without exception planning to leave the day after the wedding, we made sure to be up and about in sufficient time for us to drive to the various places where our families and guest were housed to bid them farewell and thank them for sharing in our happy day. It was only then we discovered there was dissent and disapproval. I knew that Buck had wanted us to delay our wedding. Mary Jo belatedly expressed disapproval and refused to attend the wedding. Dottie's son and daughter-in-law refused to greet us when we called their room from the lobby of the motel where they were staying. They announced they preferred not to see us, and remained in bed. We were sorrowed by these actions, but all eventually came to approve of our marriage. Others of both families expressed both their approval and support. Among those approving was Susan, perhaps the most knowledgeable and experienced of all in matrimonial matters.

HOLLAND(10)
A Month with Long Time Friends

Our dear friend, Lynn Counihan, had died in Holland a few months before Lory's death. Shortly after the second of these events probably in November of that year, Jerry Counihan, Lynn's husband, called to announce that he was traveling a bit and was presently in Florida. "Would it be OK if I came for a visit?" he inquired by phone.

I leaped at the opportunity and responded, "Come and stay with me long as you can. I'll enjoy every minute of it." Jerry's response indicated his schedule was such that he could only stay for two nights, but it was a great opportunity to catch up on the happenings in our respective lives. We exchanged a few further comments and I informed him of my intention to marry Dottie.

On the first evening of Jerry's visit I fixed a rice and curry dinner, Dottie joined us and we three enjoyed a great evening, with Dottie contributing enthusiastically to the conversation. We each had a couple of cocktails and in the afterglow we told Jerry our plans to be married in January and of our plan to make a trip to Holland in May to visit other old friends of mine and expose Dottie to Tulip Time.

In addition, I also had a need to travel to Baldwin, Michigan, about a hundred miles north of Holland to do something about a problem with a forty acre parcel if land I owned near a lake several miles from the town. The property had been sold on a land contract, but in violation of the terms of the contract the buyers had not been regular in their monthly payments and on several occasions had not made the scheduled payment at all. Something had to be done to correct this situation. I knew and liked the people who were buying the property but could not acquiesce to their level of performance. I knew they had had financial difficulties before. I wanted to help, but couldn't allow the situation to deteriorate further.

In his turn, Jerry told of a forthcoming visit he was going to make to Ireland and Italy. "I'm going to be gone for six weeks," he said, "So I'll be leaving just before the beginning of Tulip Time, and you are welcome to stay in the house for as much of that period as you care to. You can be house sitters, do a few minor repairs around the house and occasionally mow the lawn during my absence."

This generous offer was one impossible to resist. Jerry would be leaving a day or so before our arrival so he left the keys with a mutual friend who lived nearby and we picked them up when we got there in May.

The Counihan house was a four bedroom brick ranch style dwelling of the type that was particularly popular in the nineteen fifties. It was fully equipped; all we had to do was buy our groceries and other supplies as necessary.

We scheduled ourselves to make the most of our time. As a former member and president of the Holland Rotary Club, as well as governor of the Rotary district that extended northward from Holland to Wawa, Ontario in Canada I was anxious to make up attendance weekly at my old club and renew contacts with many of my friends. We made free use of Jerry's phone to contact old friends and arrange to spend some time with those who were available. We toured the campus of Hope College, my alma mater, and the campus of Holland High School where I had served as a teacher and later as the principal for a period of twenty years.

One day we toured Baywoodlands, the subdivision Lory and I had developed upon my retirement from the navy, dropped in on a couple of former neighbors and then drove through the beautiful Waukazoo area and Ottawa Beach State Park before stopping for lunch at the Ottawa Beach Inn, now operated by a former student of mine.

When Tulip Time began we sat on the curb in front of the

Woolworth store and watched the street scrubbing, a traditional part of the opening parade. In the late afternoon we stood at the edge of Centennial Park across from the post office and watched a hundred or more high school girls costumed in traditional authentic Dutch attire dance in groups performing the klompen dance. The sound of their wooden shoes pounding on the pavement in unison permeated the scene. Whether by choice or accident, several girls' shoes flew off their feet while doing the high kicks that are part of the dance routine. It was a great week, ending with the annual band parade involving thirty bands from around the state.

Our time in Michigan was passing quickly and we decided we would drive to Baldwin the following Monday to attend to the bit of business I had there involving the sale of one of the last pieces of property I owned in Michigan, a square forty acres near one of the many lakes in the Baldwin area. The sole remaining property, also in the Baldwin area was a two bedroom cottage on the Manistee River a couple of miles out of town.

I had sold the forty acre parcel on land contract to a couple who promised much, but often missed their payments. They were taking advantage, it seemed, of the distance between Baldwin and my Florida residence and also my inattention to this particular matter as a result of the constant burden on my time that accompanied Lory's long illness and other distracting events.

I had been ready to obtain a court order for the eviction of the purchasers but things then took a turn for the better.

It was often difficult to contact these people. They lived in a mobile home they had placed on the property, an additional violation of the provision in the land contract prohibiting the purchaser from building or living on the property without the specific written permission of the seller.

Apparently they were frequently absent, didn't answer the phone and didn't have an answering machine, but early in our Holland visit I reached them, thinking that I would once again get a set of evasive answers leading me to the point where court action would be required, a move I really didn't want to take. To my surprise, the husband said after a rather elaborate introduction to the subject, "We've arranged to pay you off anytime you can get here during banking hours. Let us know when you can get here."

Without hesitation I replied, "We'll be there Monday morning and will plan to meet you at the Osceola State Bank at ten." I gave the man Jerry's phone number and asked that he call if it was necessary to change plans.

It was a pleasant drive to Baldwin. We met the buyers at the bank as planned, all went well and very shortly we were handed a certified check for the proceeds. The purchasers then urged us to join them for lunch at the Baldwin Diner, a favorite of mine and apparently a favorite of our would-be hosts; an institution across the street from the bank that specialized in rugged family style food. We talked for some time and I found these folks to be far from the demons I had envisioned them to be.

They told of the difficult lives they had had, the loss of jobs, the raising of children and finally their purchase of the property as a place where they could start a business breeding, raising and training horses. It seemed every other sentence contained an apology for their past delinquencies and I felt comfortable assuring them no further apologies were necessary. After all, I had a certified check in my pocket to assuage my previous anger.

After lunch we settled for a couple of double dip cones at Baldwin's "world famous" ice cream shop boasting fifty-two varieties of ice cream, and then drove the short distance out of town to my fishing cottage on the Manistee River. The stop had a dual purpose; I wanted to show the place to Dottie, but I also wanted to pick up a framed collage left by the man who had lived there until he died..

The previous owner was a retired U. S. Army Air Force pilot who had been among those who had flown one of the planes during an extensive good will visit to Central and South American capitals in the early nineteen twenties. In the course of the visits the pilots were awarded medals by the governments of all countries visited and my predecessor at the cottage had framed his awards together with citations he had received during that historic venture. That circuitous tour was quite a feat for those early days of military flying, an event that took place about the time I was born.

My intention was to preserve these historic objects from the invaders who broke into the little house quite regularly, and I also had the good intention of gifting them to the U. S. Air Force Museum or Archives, believing them to be of considerable historical value and of rather great significance to that organization.

On a subsequent visit with out daughter, Susan, then stationed in the Washngton area as an army nurse, I set out to deliver the artifacts to the appropriate air force organization. After a number of calls and being shunted around from one section to another, I finally spoke to a person who seemed to understand my intent. She indicated she would deliver them to the proper recipient. I hauled the whole to the pentagon, passed through what seemed like innumerable check points and finally arrived at the office I had called. The secretary behind the desk didn't move to help me, but indicated that the colonel would be busy for the rest of the day. "What should I do with these artifacts I have carefully preserved,?" I asked.

"Put them in the corner there. I'll tell the colonel you brought them." I had had the foresight to write a couple of sentences describing why I thought the materials were of historic significance and should be preserved. I added my address and phone number, expecting at least some acknowledgment of my contribution. I'm still waiting, but don't any longer expect anything. I wish I had kept them rather than risk the possibility that they were misappropriated, lost or stolen.

*****   *****   *****

We continued our visit to "my ol' stompin' grounds in Holland. On Sunday morning after we attended an early service at Beechwood Reformed Church, the church to which Lory and I had belonged to for years, I picked up a *Grand Rapids Press* at the drug store and sat down with a cup of coffee to read the paper, starting with my somewhat quixotic habit of turning to the classified ads prior to reading the news or feature sections, scanning first the real estate section and then "Articles for Sale". Under the latter category was an item that as a stamp collector caught my immediate attention: "For Sale, a large quantity of postage stamps, mostly used." The ad gave a phone number and I called forthwith to get details such as the size of the collection, the asking price and where the stamps could be seen.

The responses I received to my initial questions were a little astonishing, "Price? We don't know the price. The stamps don't belong to us. We brought them up from Texas after my brother's funeral. His wife asked us to take them and see what we could get for them on her behalf. You asked how they are mounted. Well, mostly they're not mounted, whatever that means. Quantity? Well, they're in paper bags and cardboard boxes, mostly with the paper bags inside the boxes."

I broke into this soliloquy to inquire, "How many boxes are there and how big are the boxes?"

"Well they're in big toilet paper boxes," he replied. They're sitting on an eight foot shelf in our laundry room and we use the shelf when we're doing our laundry, so we would like to get them out of there. Why doncha come by and take a look?"

He gave an address in a suburb of Grand Rapids and some additional directions. "We'll be there tomorrow morning about ten o'clock,: I said.

It was just before ten when we entered the driveway of the split level house at the address I had received. The owners greeted us as we opened the car door and led the way to the lower level of the house where they told us the stamps were stored temporarily. When they opened the door of the laundry room and I could focus on the scene, I could hardly believe my eyes, as our host said, "There they are, just as I said." There were nine immense corrugated toilet paper cartons, some on the twelve foot shelf and some on an adjoining table.

I stepped over to the first box to take a look. In my immediate view were dozens of paper bags filled with stamps, four or five small stamp albums and a box of stamp collectors' equipments such as tongs, hinges, watermark detectors, perforation gauges, packages of glassine envelopes and a bunch of paper clips. On the shelf interspersed with those mammoth corrugated boxes were more paper bags of stamps. Looking at these I found that while some bags contained a mixture of worldwide stamps, others contained hundreds, or even thousands of duplicates of the same stamp. I quickly looked at the several boxes and saw that their contents were similar.

I had been on many wild goose chases following similar want ads, only to find that they led to something a child had put together from stuff that had arrived in the mail, plus an admixture of merchants' green stamps and other stickers all pasted in an old notebook, the whole having no value at all. Again, I asked for a price. "Dunno," was the answer, "Whadd'll you gimmee? I told my sister I'd git rid of the stamps and send her whatever money I git."

I decided to make a low ball offer and said, "I'll give you two hundreds bucks for the lot."

"I was hoping to send at least two hundred and fifty dollars to my widowed sister in Texas," he replied.

I expected a counter offer, so in return I said, "OK, I'll pay that much, but you'll have to take a check for the two fifty. I don't have that much cash with me." My checking account was with United Services Automobile Association, an organization originally formed to provide automobile insurance for military officers at favorable rates, and hence its name, although it had expanded its businesses to include banking, credit cards and other financial matters. I then described USAA as best I could and once again asked him to accept my check.

"No check unless it's on a Grand Rapids bank." he replied. I really couldn't blame him. He was carrying out a fiduciary responsibility for his sister and didn't want to fail her. Further, he didn't know me or my background so I could understand his position, but what should I do?

I asked for the name of his bank and where the nearest branch was located. He volunteered to accompany me to the bank and introduced me to the bank officer in charge of the branch. I explained my dilemma and she indicated she might be able to help, although she had never heard of USAA.

I always carry in my wallet card with a few of the important USAA toll free numbers, and almost immediately, with the lady Grand Rapids banker on the phone, I established contact with the USAA bank and was soon talking to the appropriate official there in San Antonio. After giving many identifying names, numbers and other matters associated with my account, all of which gave the lady banker increased confidence in my reliability, USAA wired the required funds to the Grand Rapids bank and the lady behind the desk delivered a certified check to my new friend.

We proceeded to load that mother lode of stamps into the trunk and back seat my four-door Cadillac. With some adjustments we got them all on board and they filled both spaces. I would be able to sort stamps for the rest of my life and still have some unsorted ones left over.

After some adjustment to the contents of those boxes to make maximum use of space, I taped them all shut and called Federal Express to pick tem up and deliver them to Stuart. The shipping cost was almost half of what I had paid for the lot.

Now, as I write this tale, my active stamp collecting has come to an end. I am still interested in stamps and hoard anything of a philatelic nature that falls into my purview, but I could no longer lift the massive albums involved and I have thus sold most of my foreign collection. In the negotiation for the sale I held back a couple of those brown paper bags loaded with stamps. They are sitting in our storage locker here in Sandhill Cove just in case I get the urge once again to sort some of the contents, looking for the treasure that could possibly be there.

Our memorable trip to Holland was over and we drove onward to the shack for the summer.

STENOSIS (11)

Paralyzed

At Christmas time we made another attempt to spend at least some of the holiday period at the shack. We would fly together to North Carolina, where Dottie would join her son and family for the holiday. I would fly to Norfolk and spend a few days with son Buck and his growing family. Neither family visit was entirely successful, and we had only limited time at the shck. As a result we resolved to find more satisfactory ways to spend the November and December holidays.

We enjoyed a pleasant summer at the shack, where I undertook the first step toward the pruning of the spruce plantings covering about ten acres at the top of the hill overlooking the shack, its meadow and the two creeks bounding the whole scene. At summer's end we returned to our house in Stuart, but planned to venture northward to Wells Tannery for the December holidays and several planned affairs there with our many friends in the valley.

It was a week before our intended departure by automobile when I wakened one morning, sat on the edge of the bed and tried to raise my arms above my head. I tried repeatedly while suffering considerable pain during my attempts, but could not get my hands above my shoulders. I went to see the doctor who had served us during Lory's final illness and after a cursory examination, he said, "You've just strained some muscles," and wrote prescriptions for a relaxant and something for the pain. I took the medicines regularly, but sensed no improvement. Despite the warning indications we were determined to proceed with our plans.

During the fifteen hundred mile drive to the shack I was comfortable riding along behind the wheel as Dottie snoozed beside me. Our overnight stop in North Carolina was most pleasant and the dinner we ordered in the adjoining restaurant was so good we resolved to stop there in the future. I was a bit stiff in the morning, but felt better after breakfast and we made an early start. There was very little snow, even in the mountains. We arrived in the early evening and found our friend Ron had turned up the heat, so all was cozy in the shack. We fixed a dinner from a few supplies we had brought with us and crawled into that spacious second floor bed.

We invited our many Wells Valley friends for open house on Christmas Day. This required a trip to Bedford for supplies. I was miserable the whole time, and on our return found I could carry only a few of the groceries into the house. Dottie decorated the place while I held a hot pad on my shoulders and complained. I suffered through the open house and the following week. I took my prescribed medicines regularly and prayed for the best. On New Year's Eve morning I fell on the floor in the dining room and couldn't get up. Dottie called Ron and he came over and hoisted me to my feet. I was starting to feel that something was seriously wrong with me.

A progressive dinner was planned for New Years Eve with portions of the meal to be served in various houses, each several miles apart in the Valley. In recognition of my increasing disability Ward and Rosemary Woodall, members of the Moseby clan, picked us up and drove us to the various dinner sites.

The finale was dessert at the home of Bill and Caroline Moseby, an impressive house with a mammoth living room filled with the artifacts and commendations collected during Bill's long career in the Central Intelligence Agency. In the midst of this final gathering, I fell on the floor once more and had to be hoisted to my feet. One of the participants was our minister at the Wells Valley Church who offered to pray for me, and I replied, "Any port in a storm, pastor." He prayed on my behalf, but this didn't seem to ease my problem or the accompanying mental tension. The nearest physician was at least thirty miles away across the mountains.

Searching for some succor, my mind scoured the possibilities, and my thoughts finally came to rest on the only physician I knew other than the quack who had misdiagnosed my case in the first place. Fortunately I had with me a copy of the *Rota-Sail,* the weekly bulletin of the Stuart Rotary Club and it listed phone numbers for all members of the club. From it I picked out the name of Carlos Maldenado, a cardiovascular surgeon, whose residence phone number was listed as well as his professional number. Assuming he would not be available through his office, I called the home number and got his answering machine.

In a rather long message, recognizing that my case did not fall within his specialty, I attempted to explain my increasingly desperate situation, my symptoms, and asked for whatever help or recommendation he could offer. While waiting and praying for a response, seeking a little diversion from this increasingly difficult situation, we turned on the television in the old living room now serving as a combination guest bedroom and TV room. A weather bulletin greeted us. A winter storm warning was issued for all points north of the Carolinas and east of Ohio projecting freezing rain followed by snow. We would be trapped in the valley for days if we didn't leave in time to avoid this frontal storm; we wouldn't even be able to start up the mountain on those steep grades if they were covered with ice.

The phone rang. It was Dr. Maldanado.

Reacting to the information I had left on his answering machine, he said, "Fritz, you must get back here to Stuart as fast as you can by any means that you can. You have a stenosis somewhere in your spine and we have the best team of orthopedic surgeons in the country to take care of that problem right here at Martin Memorial. I will contact them first thing in the morning and tell them you are coming. If this condition isn't corrected forthwith you will lose all mobility." He gave me the phone number of the office of Doctors Afshar and Robinson.

We gathered our things, gave a call to Ron asking him to winterize and close the shack. With that we got into the car, hoping to get at least to the top of the mountain before contacting ice and freezing rain. I was relatively comfortable in the driver's seat, but increasingly conscious of my desperate situation. We made it to the top and pressed onward for the many hours required to insure we were south of the storm track before turning in for the night. Another long day of driving took us to Stuart and the following morning I called the office of the recommended orthopedic surgeons, Drs. Afshar and Robinson.

Their examination confirmed what Dr. Maldonado had told me. They determined that the stenosis was of my C-3 through C-6 vertebrae and scheduled me for surgery early on. Meanwhile, I would have to have a pre-operation physical examination by a general practitioner to reveal my overall physical condition.

I could only turn to the physician who had earlier misdiagnosed me. He had all my records. At least I was given a speedy appointment in recognition of my urgent need. We called Susan, my oldest daughter and asked her to fly down and help Dottie with the post operative care I was going to need. At least I would have two high powered registered nurses taking acre of me during my recovery.

I was lying on the operating table under an anesthesia that left me conscious and the surgeons talked to me frequently as they performed their delicate functions. I later learned they had sawed off the back half of the identified vertebrae and replaced the now missing bone with a titanium plate and screws plus some permanent glue. With great care they installed a collar on me, and warned me not to move anything above the waist other than my eyeballs. To further insure immobility my head was fixed to my shoulders with enough tape to tape up a football team before a game. I was very gently hoisted into bed and I fell asleep immediately.

Consciousness returned when I sensed that people were standing next to the bed. To my astonishment they were Les and Elaine, Dottie's cousins. What were they doing there? They were in Stuart en route for a winter stay in Florida and somehow found out I was in the hospital under intensive care. They were only allowed to stay for few minutes and then left.

Dottie and Susan arrived. They had gone shopping to pass the time during my surgery and had returned. My first mumbled message to them was "Les and Elaine just left." They thought I was delusional, but when the couple later called to announce their presence in Stuart, my statement was accepted as the truth.

Evidently there were many cases of communicable diseases in the hospital, and recognizing I would have two registered nurses caring for me, the doctors decided to send me home by ambulance the next day. I was handled like a case of eggs and placed in an easy chair in the living room of the shack facing the television with a urinal I could reach without straining.

I sat in that chair in that position for several months, frightened that all would be lost if I moved any thing above my shoulders except my eyeballs. At last I was carried to bed and placed on my back, from which position I could stare only at the ceiling. Eventually I was able to get up and renew a fairly normal life, albeit with that damnable collar holding my head up and locked in place.

ADJUSTMENTS & HONEYMOONS (12)
"Each Must Give One Hundred Percent"

There were some attempts to interest me in golf. I tried, but could only frustrate others playing with me. I could get on the green quite readily but usually used six or eight putts to hole the ball. My conclusions on golf could be summarized as follows:

(1) The game spoils an otherwise good walk;

(2) Golf could better be played indoors on a pool table;

(3) Most golfers could not compete with the pros, so why try?

(4) Sailing is far more fun.

As to sailing, it was not Dottie's cup of tea just as golf was not mine. Ken Horsburgh, the fellow from Cleveland to whom I had sold my Ensign class boat when we moved to Florida, now wintered in a subdivision across the river from Miles Grant. He kept his boat at The Dock a restaurant and marina enterprise located about equidistant from our houses. Ken would often seek a crewman to go with him on a sail around the north fork of the St. Lucie River, and I was usually ready to go with him

Dottie's experience with the water had been limited to swimming in a club pool, occasional canoeing and riding in a pontoon boat during the cocktail hour.

Was she looking for someone to defeat at golf? Was I looking for someone who was not intimidated by the art of sailing? Ken scotched any hope I might have had that Dottie would learn to like boating when he invited us for a ride in his light but overpowered planing speed boat. We met on schedule at the marina where the boat was kept in dry storage. As usual with any such appointment, Ken was early on the scene, had the boat in the water and was ready to go.

It was low tide and a bit difficult getting Dottie into the boat at all, but we managed. She mentioned to Ken that she was fearful of fractures due to the fact she had osteoporosis. He acknowledged her comment, but I doubt he understood her concern. With Dottie seated between us Ken motored slowly out through the marina channel onto the broader waters of the St. Lucie where he gunned the engine and we took off like a rocket headed for the "No Wake" zone in the water approach to the railroad bridge and the new US-1 highway bridge. Dottie screamed most of the way until Ken pulled back the throttle for a peaceful trip under the bridges.

It must have been that Ken interpreted her screams as expressions of combined pleasure and enthusiasm rather than signs of fear that her vertebrae would be crushed. Once cleared of the slow zone we rocketed once more down the St. Lucie toward the junction of the St. Lucie and Indian Rivers en route to the channel out to the ocean, passing as we went the hospital, the dock at Pierpoint on our right and Frances Langford's estate on our left, with Dottie screaming the entire route of several miles.

At Sand Sprit Park just inside the channel to the ocean we were once more in a no wake zone and idled along in relative peace. "We'll just take a peak outside," announced Ken as we headed out through the channel to the ocean, once more gliding along smoothly over the protected waters between the breakwaters. "Not bad at all," Ken stated as we emerged into the Atlantic. It really wasn't bad as such matters go; the long ocean waves were running a mere three feet or so. "Here we go!" yelled Ken as he pushed the throttle forward one more time.

Once on the step the boat leaped from wave crest to wave crest landing with a slap on each successive wave. It was sheer horror for Dottie and a delight for Ken. Fortunately he decided that his allotted time for boating that day was about up, and we headed back into more sheltered waters. We finally made it back to The Dock, Ken's favorite waterside restaurant where we each grilled a steak and Dottie and I each had a cocktail. Ken, a teetotaler, had a glass of milk. Responding to a plea from Dottie

Ken agreed to idle our way back to the marina. I now more fully realized why Ken's wife, Ruth, refused to get into a boat with Ken for any reason whatsoever.

As to golf, I sincerely tried to enjoy the game, and did have some success, in a way. Somewhat against my will, I agreed to take a few lessons from the pro at Miles Grant. He was successful in teaching me to hold a driver in a way that would minimize the number of deviant balls to cuts and slices. Miles Grant was an executive course with short fairways and I could often get on the green in two or three strokes. A major problem was that I never could learn to putt. I could be on the green or just off it in the two or three strokes, but then take a dozen strokes to hole out. I drove me fellow players nuts.

Eventually when we were moving from the Miles Grant area we contributed our clubs to Miles Grant, hoping that someone else could us them more successfully than I had,

<u>HAWAII</u>(13)
"You Can Never Go Back"

Almost immediately after our wedding we were made aware of the fact that several of our adult children disapproved of our decision to be married. This surprised, disappointed, hurt and mystified us, since several of the disapprovers, in their time, had fallen in love and married without seeking our approval. That having been said, in an extension of our reactions, we concluded that we would not impose on the activities of any of our children during the Thanksgiving to New Year's holiday season, as any time spent with one might upset all. Rather, we decided, we would do something adventurous on our own each year, and, it was hoped, upset no one.

"The reunion of Pearl Harbor survivors is an annual event held in various places across the country, but every fifth year on the anniversary of the Japanese attack, it is held in Hawaii," I remarked one evening, "And this is a year for Hawaii."

Dottie told me about a budding romance she had once had with a young man who ultimately moved to Hawaii' "I thought I would never want to go there after that, but now that I've met you and heard more about their wonders, I guess I would like to visit the islands." It was thus, after a few more discussions of the matter, we decided to spend the second holiday season following our marriage in Hawaii, starting with the reunion of the Pearl Harbor veterans on the sixtieth anniversary of the attack, and then continuing our visit for five weeks to be devoted to exploring some of the islands.

"Lest we forget," were words that did not ring true in my mind, except as sarcasm, after attending a previous gathering of the Pearl Harbor Survivors in Honolulu during a year in which the anniversary of the Japanese attack fell once again on Sunday. To the dismay of the assembled attack survivors, the Honolulu Marathon was planned, not only on the anniversary of the attack, but was also scheduled to include the seven fifty-five a.m. time when the survivors' memorial service was to begin at the Punchbowl National Cemetery, where hundreds of Pacific war dead are buried.

The result, despite objections, was that the Marathon prevailed, and we "survivors" were forced to rise at four o'clock, chomp on a doughnut and swig a bit of coffee from a plastic cup while standing in line to board the busses for The Punchbowl if we were to attend the memorial service. "Some days you never forget," a sentence imbedded in every Pearl Harbor Survivor's mind, fit this occasion as well. I had resolved at that time never to suffer such an indignity again.

But time does change perceptions, and tt was thus, after a few more discussions of the matter, we decided to spend the second holiday season following our marriage in Hawaii, starting with the reunion of the Pearl Harbor veterans on the sixtieth anniversary of the attack, and then continuing our visit for five weeks to be devoted to exploring several of the islands.

The long flight from West Palm Beach to Hawaii came to an end at three-thirty in the afternoon, Hawaiian time, and we were greeted by hula dancers who garlanded us with leis as a light rain fell, and a rainbow shone over the mountains to the north. During the taxi ride through busy downtown Honolulu streets en route to Waikiki, Dottie remarked, "This place is as busy as Chicago!" It was busy all right and nothing like the pre-war and wartime Honolulu I had experienced before. We settled into the glitzy Ala Moana Hotel, the skyscraper reunion headquarters, for the three day affair to begin a couple of days after our arrival. For me this hotel had none of the romance or glamour of the colonial Moana whose charms I had enjoyed a few times both before and during the war.

My collection of Hawaiian aloha shirts from previous visits was entirely adequate, but Dottie required a muumuu to be in conformity at the evening's performance of the Polynesian Dinner Theater, so we scoured the equally glitzy Ala Moana Shopping Center for just the right one.

The reunion was hardly remarkable. The busses to the Punchbowl were late and then for some bureaucratic reason, they were required to take a devious route. As a result, Pearl Harbor Survivors, in whose recognition the event was scheduled, missed the opening ceremonies that were scheduled to include the 7:55 a.m. time of the Pearl Harbor attack. Further, we were relegated to seats well to the rear, and many were required to stand during the service, while children and curious adults occupied the front seating that presumably was to be reserved for us. Our treatment was the exact opposite of what we might have expected. I was further irritated by the fact that there were not enough printed programs available for us as late comers, while children up toward the speakers' platform were sailing them around as paper airplanes. I picked up a couple of them off the ground to be included among my memorabilia

The parade of "survivors" down Kalakaua Avenue, an event that had been a feature of these reunions since their beginning was one of "the lame, the halt and the blind," with many of the survivors in wheel chairs, using walkers or supported by canes. I reminded myself that sailors on liberty often called this street Cow-Cow Avenue.

The banquet was a mass of humanity made memorable for me by three things: First, it was a beautiful meal, but the survivor next to me complained that his gigantic filet was "too rare." I happily accepted it and wrapped it in a napkin to provide for some of our needs in ensuing days. Second, my meal was interrupted when I was called from the banquet room to respond to a request from the National Park Service to give my version of what happened to me on that fateful December days fifty years before. Third was a memorable speech by Sam Donaldson, the news commentator, and then, finally, I had the opportunity to eat my dinner, which by then was cold, while everyone else present was enjoying dessert.

The next day we moved our belongings to a room overlooking the ocean in the beautiful new Hale Koa hotel an establishment built with funds contributed from profits made on sales in exchanges of the armed services. The hotel was built on the site of the former Fort deRussy, a location that has more ocean frontage than any of the other Waikiki hotels and its use is restricted to members of the armed forces, both active and retired, and their families. Its expanse is a relief from the rest of Waikiki in that it landscaped and rather natural as a park. All else is paved over, a radical change from the Waikiki I had known.

Our room overlooking both ocean and mountains was spacious and well furnished. The hotel's two lobbies and all public areas were extravagantly decorated for the holiday season and featured a model railroad running through the whole with piles of Santa's gifts aboard the cars. Christmas music was everywhere. Garlands, tinsel, ginger bread houses, flocked trees, manikins, Christmas lighting and other Christmas decorations were everywhere in public spaces. Several additional toy trains made their way throughout the whole

The next day was Sunday and we traveled to the nearby Presbyterian Church making the short trip aboard the Fort deRussy shuttle titled "The deRussy Caboose" and were slightly surprised when the minister, a navy chaplain asked all survivors and spouses to stand and be recognized. A group of perhaps fifteen rose and were greeted with a round of applause by the parishioners. Afterward we enjoyed the fellowship of other worshippers as we munched on appetizers provided by members of the congregation. Several invited us to their homes during our visit, but that was deemed impossible because of the demands of our schedules.

On Monday after an exploratory bus ride through the jungle of Waikiki and out to Diamond Head Beach Park, we walked along the beach back to the original Moana Hotel, where we had lunch in the Banyan Court, and I retold the story of my pre-war swing across the court from the top of the hotel lanai on a banyan air root, across the table of my shipmate and mentor, Al Shephard, and his date. It was for this act Mr. Shephard awarded me an informal restriction to the ship for the following weekend, and it was thus I was on board the ship at the time of the attack on Pearl Harbor.

We spent the week exploring Oahu visiting tourist attractions and places where I had spent some leisure time many years before. Diamond Head and Koko came under our surveillance and we made a short stop at the Blow Hole to watch the impressive spurt of ocean come up out of the lava rock. The officers' club at the Marine Corps Base at Kailua was our stop for lunch, and then visited the Kailua Yacht Club briefly and exerted our exchange reciprocity, although we didn't actually do anything except exchange a few comments with several members who happened to be present.

As we drove northward Dottie was surprised to see the large herds of cattle, sheep, goats and horses. We spent an hour on the north side of the island watching the skilled surfers perform in the record high waves, and then turned back at Haleiwa through groves of papaya and then through vast field of pineapples past the Dole processing plant, Fort Shafter and finally home to the Hale Koa. It had been another long day.

We repeated some of our east coast driving and the climb up over the Pali. What is this about Hawaii Interstate One? How can there be an Interstate within a single state? Beyond that, one evening was devoted to a Hawaiian luau on the grounds of Fort deRussy. The roast pig, native fruits and other servings were excellent, but the poi still tasted like library paste. The music and hula dancers were as good as ever.

Our journal continues, "Drove up the west coast to Makaha and had a picnic lunch of pork sandwiches, raisins and water. We were quite tired and Dottie's leg was becoming painful from all the walking so we rested for a time, after which we made our way to the Barefoot Bar and had a drink while listening to Hawaiian music by one Lopaka Brown and his group."

The next two days, our last on Oahu, were rainy with heavy winds, so we stayed close to Hale Koa, where there was plenty of entertainment including a performance by a choral group composed of Hale Koa employees and a recital by a skilled harpist. Among other things, we were trying to keep the strain off Dottie's leg.

Getting underway on Saturday proved once again to be quite a challenge. We pulled everything together and loaded the whole into the rental car. As we struggled through Honolulu traffic, I commented to Dottie, "It takes longer to get to the airport than it does to get to the next island." We finally made it to the airport, turned in our car and forced ourselves through what seemed like a human zoo to get to Hawaiian Air. "We passed long lines for all Hawaiian Air mainland destinations and then found ourselves in a long line for the inter island destinations check in counter. Next we stood in an equally long line to board the plane. This was our first experience with first come, first served seating, but we managed to get adjoining seats. Each of these waits was longer than our actual flight time to Hilo.

"It was quite a hike from the gate to our rental car, but we were soon on our way covering the twenty-eight miles to the Kilauea Armed Forces Recreational Camp on the fringe of Hawaii's Volcano National Park, where we would stay for the next ten days while exploring the island. Once again our qualification to use the facilities of the camp was a perk that came with my service connection.

"We kept a hand-written journal and much of the following is taken directly from it. "The check-in was easy, but on approach to our cabin we suffered a blowout of the left front tire when I scraped a curb while peering out the window trying to determine whether the cabin I was looking at in the dusk was ours. The cabin turned out to be the one to which we were assigned. I changed the tire and we settled down in a beautiful cabin, one of a number that had been built in the nineteen twenties by an investment group that planned to profit from tourists coming to view the volcano after which the park is named. The cabin and its accoutrements appeared to be the best available at the time it was built. The bathroom was fitted with a black marble Jacuzzi larger than some peoples' swimming pools. Following the company's failure, its property was purchased by *the government and added to the Volcano National Park property.*

"By the time we were settled in we were too tired to search out what we later found to be a well stocked commissary, so for dinner we heated a can of Spaghetti-O's we had carried with us. There was a gas stove in the kitchen. Bed beckoned us early.

"It was cold and rain poured down all night, but after breakfast, We took the Crater Rim Drive around the Kilauea Calder and stopped several times at scenic overlooks at each of which we were properly amazed at the vastness of the volcano. Although Dottie's knee was bothering her, we stopped at the Jaggar Museum and overlook. After completing the circuit we took the Chain of Craters road to the point along the coast where lava from a recent eruption had poured over it blocking further travel. On the return we stopped at the commissary and bought chicken, green beans and potatoes for the dinner Fritz prepared. Our evening entertainment was our regular cribbage game, which Dottie won.

"It was pouring again all night and showed no sign of letting up, so we decided to go to the Kona Coast to dry out. For lunch we split a yellow fin tuna sandwich at a second floor restaurant right over the water and watched a cruise ship come in to anchor. We then continued around the island until we got to the headquarters of the famous Parker ranch and further to Waimea, a nice town," we noted.

"After lunch, we continued to Waipio Lookout, a much greater distance than we had anticipated, and stopped at the state park where the road comes to an end. The park was filled to capacity with cars, people and numerous chickens. The surf was up and shortly after we turned around to head back to Hilo we ran into some flooding across the road and then passed houses with beautiful gardens, some with cattle, horses and goats and one ranch with a large flock of sheep.

I wanted to see the area called Hawaiian Acres, a large and mostly undeveloped subdivision lying south and southwesterly from Kurtistown because I had once owned a six acre parcel there. Before leaving home I had looked for the plat map of the area, but had been unable to find it. The only road we could find that led into the area soon dwindled into a muddy unpaved track. We passed several very nice looking homes and one fairly large fenced tract planted with nursery stock. The rest of the land around us was filled with brushy undergrowth. My thought was, "How did they manage to survey this place as a subdivision?"

We finally arrived at an intersection of the rutted one lane tracks. At this point there was a tall post with a sign about ten feet off the ground with an arrow pointing to our right and an inscription reading, 'Hawaiian Acres Clubhouse.' Despite my desire to see the clubhouse, I looked down the muddy track to which the sign pointed and lost my courage. We finally turned around, found our way to the main road, bought a newspaper in Hilo and headed back to our quarters.

At this point "Dottie the Nurse," who had spent much of her career in care of the elderly, took over the planning for the next day. She spotted an ad for a nursing home in the paper, and thus motivated, went to the phone book in the cabin and found two more nursing homes advertised in the yellow pages. From the three she picked the largest, advertised as the second largest in the state, for her visit. We drove to the facility and I was left in the car for a nap while Dottie visited for a couple of hours.

Her record of the visit says, "I entered the nursing home via a large slate floored open lanai and asked at the desk to see the director of nursing. Meanwhile I read the state license, the facility's federal certification and awards for having no deficiencies all displayed on a wall near the front desk. Shortly the director of nursing, Allyson Andrews-Nelson, a registered nurse certified in geriatrics, appeared and took me on a tour of the three story building, answering my questions freely as we visited the various areas of the facility. She was a very vivacious and friendly person, obviously in love with her job. She exuded enthusiasm as she described her innovative methods of providing for infection control and staff motivation. 'Many employees have been on the staff for fifteen or more years and most are related to residents,' she said, speaking in friendly terms to each passing employee. All wear facility-provided waist support braces. As we finished the tour and I was saying my farewell, a group of volunteer female dancers appeared in Santa Claus costumes and danced on each floor for the entertainment of the residents."

After breakfast the next day, my narrative continues, "We set out to explore State Road 130 to the east side of the lava flow that had blocked out way earlier and then around the eastern shore below Hilo. The area was rather isolated, with only a few scattered houses along the way. We stopped for lunch at a place overlooking the ocean where there was room to park and then continued our journey taking the left fork of an intersection, and left the route along and above the ocean. The paved road ended, and eventually we found ourselves driving on a single rutted road. We knew we were going north toward Hilo, but began to have doubts as to where we were going in the meantime.

"About then a three-car convoy came from the opposite direction. We tried to flag them down, but only the last vehicle a four-wheel drive van stopped. The woman driver, who had three small children with her, strongly advised us to reverse course and take that right fork we had ignored earlier, a continuation of State Road 130. So back we went and scooted safely back to our cabin.

"The next day, Thursday, after our usual camp breakfast we gassed at the camp pump and departed for Saddle Road. Our inquiries about this road, which crosses the island through the lava fields brought forth the following comments: 'There is no connecting road short of Hilo,' and 'The road is very steep, narrow, twisting and dangerous and not recommended for tourists or casual visitors. As it turned out we had no difficulty in finding the road. It was paved and quite wide for a secondary road. It was steep with sharp curves for several short distances, but none was as steep, sharp or long as the roads in the mountains of Central Pennsylvania.

"After the climb up to a relatively level area our path lay across lava field where little or nothing grows, but with spectacular views of both Mauna Loa and Mauna Kea. The latter was largely free of clouds and topped with snow. Beyond the lava we entered an army maneuvering area and drove on a rough poorly maintained single lane road until we came to a sign announcing we were entering the Parker Ranch and the road improved markedly for the next seven miles before we reaching SR250 toward Hawi. We then began climbing, climbing, climbing through areas containing herds of cattle and sheep and then downward on paved road to sea level. When we reached the ocean it was a long drive home via the Kona Coast, South Point and so forth. We were tired and went to the camp cafeteria where we joined a number of camp employees for an oriental dinner.

"On Friday the twenty first we planned for a light day around the Hilo area. We ate a leisurely breakfast, started back down SR11 and stopped at the orchid gardens we had noted before and viewed a tremendous variety of the flowers, many of which we deemed to be beautiful but impressively pricey. After making our way successfully through the accompanying tourist trap store, we made our way back to the nursing home where Dottie picked up some documents and literature she had been promised by Ms. Andrews-Nelson. It was then on to Wal-Mart to buy seven boxes of chocolate covered macadamian nuts for distribution to our families.

"We drove around Hilo for a time and then as planned stopped at beautiful park on Hilo Bay a bit past the industrial park on Kalaniana Ole Avenue for lunch. There were several picnic tables under thatched roofs and we selected one where we could watch youthful Hawaiians swimming and bathing in the spring-fed salt water pools connected to Hilo Bay. We had to wait for a half hour before eating because of a pill Dottie had taken at Wal-Mart, so we sat and watched a very fat Hawaiian man mowing the grass with a weed whip. Shortly a very fat Hawaiian woman dressed in a red muumuu arrived and sat down to talk to us about a skin condition that she said was caused by a prescribed antibiotic she had taken. She then joined the young folks in the water for a therapeutic bath.

"Later, as we were eating, she and the mower joined us at the table and there was much lively conversation, including expressions by all of how beautiful this park was. The woman introduced herself as Cecelia and when we asked her last name she said, rather proudly, 'You might not believe this, but I am descended from Hawaiian royalty and my name, which I will spell for you is Hiiakaikapliopele-Samson.' She was fascinated by Fritz's blue and gave him the appellation, 'Baby blue eyes', a name she repeated many times.

"Finally we were joined by another very fat man, a school employee in the field of teaching the handicapped. All these folks, despite their short stature, we later judged, weighed close to three hundred pounds. The conversation turned back to the park in which we were sitting and much emphasis was placed on a fact we had not previously been aware of, the park is not a public park but is owned, operated and maintained by the Hawaiian community although we were welcome as guests. The other topic was how little Dottie and I had eaten. Our lunch consisted of a ham sandwich and half of a small papaya apiece. Their comment was that our papaya was not really ripe, being only slightly red, and they rarely eat them anyway, ripe or not. Finally, after many alohas the school man gave us a huge avocado, the largest I've ever seen, and we were on our way back to the cabin to pack for tomorrow's departure for Kauai.

"Saturday morning we repacked a bit and found we need ed to carry another shopping bag in addition to our regular luggage. It contained a box of Raisin Bran, seven boxes of chocolate covered macadamian nuts, the huge avocado, five pounds of Kona coffe and the plastic dishes we had bought for use at the camp. The plane for Honolulu left at eleven fifteen, and we were boarded with ease after a short wait. Honolulu was a different matter. It was a madhouse, but we managed to get to the plane departing for Lihue on time. As usual it was overbooked for the short flight to Kauai.

"Our rental car was waiting for us when we arrived and in short order we were on our way to the resort we had booked, but it was only after several reverses of course that we found it lurking well off the road behind and above the Coconut Market Place and a motel. Our suite was beautiful and well equipped with king sized bed, well equipped kitchen and a balcony overlooking the ocean beyond the Market Place. It turned out the owners were trying to sell time shares and applied strenuous pressure trying unsuccessfully to persuade us to spend part of our limited time on Kauai suffering through a sales pitch for something we didn't want." After overcoming the pressures of the time share folks we enjoyed the lavish surroundings for the few days we were there."

Dinner the first night was a place called the Bull Shed a short way down the main road from the hotel. As we entered we were greeted by a group of local residents who invited us to join them and assured us, "You're in the right place for good food, the best in Hawaii." We ordered steaks, ate well and carried enough back to the time share for two more meals.

Our first adventure the next morning was, "....to drive up east and north coasts of Kauai to the extreme end of the road at Kaulua Beach where the mountain runs to the sea, making a circle island tour all but impossible. En route we passed several beaches before the road took us inland a bit with towering mountains on our left and past farms on either side of the road, to the town of Kilauea. (Yes, another one!!)

"We took a little side trip for about a mile to visit Christ Memorial Episcopal Church, a stone structure with beautiful stained glass window and a decorated Christmas tree outside to mark the season. We then back-tracked and drove to Kilauea lighthouse, which is inside the Kilauea Point National Wildlife Refuge. This was a great experience. Parking was restricted to the lower level and we weren't sure we could make it up to the lighthouse, but a park ranger came along and offered to get us a golf cart, which soon arrived, driven by an attractive young woman who was staying with her father and step mother for a year. She said she attended high school on the island but also worked at two jobs in addition to her volunteer work at the Refuge.

"She drove us to the overlook above Crater Hill Bay where the surf is spectacular and thence up the steep path to the lighthouse. From the time we arrived in the park we were surrounded by birds, both flying and resting on the ground. Families of Nene geese (pronounced nay-nay) were everywhere. It was the first time either of us had seen the Hawaiian state bird.

"From there we drove up the steep path to the lighthouse, where we had a good view of several small offshore islets. There were telescopes set to give the viewer a look at the nests and families of albatross perched on an isolated ledge west of the light. Plaques on either side of the path described the wildlife found in the park and we stopped to read each one. This was certainly one of the highlights of our Hawaiian adventure.

"For lack of time we passed up the opportunity to visit Princeville, a modern resort community, crossed the Hanalei bridge and passed Lumaha beach before crossing the Waimaha bridge, where the road narrowed to a single lane. After passing over a number of smaller one-lane bridges, we finally came to the end of the road wjere a crowd of people were partying and picnicking. Hundred of colorful chickens ran through the crowd." We were back at our rental unit by dinner time and collapsed in bed after the meal.

"We devoted the next day, Christmas Eve, to a ride to and around the rim of the famous Waimea Canyon. To our surprise, there was sugar cane growing right up to the road on either side for much of the way. Dottie didn't enjoy this part of the ride too much and I was busy trying to figure out where we were, but finally we arrived at one of the principal lookouts in the park. When Dottie saw the many narrow steps up from the parking area to the lookout, she balked and we took in the spectacular view from the edge of the parking lot. The canyon is one mile wide, ten miles long and 3,657 feet deep.

"Christmas Day we enjoyed a delicious breakfast in the room consisting of poached eggs, orange slices and muffins plus our usual tea and coffee. We drove a mile or so to the Wailua River State Park and took the highly advertised tour boat up to the Fern Grotto. Most of the passengers were Japanese from a tour bus. There was much ukulele, guitar and vocal music. Hula dancers greeted us at the dock below the grotto and then we found hard walking up steps toward the grotto. We decided not to take the final group of steps, but rather watch the others and listen to the music. Once again, colorful bantam chickens were everywhere. A single cat sat on a rock shelf and observed the whole scene quietly. On our return to the hotel we made phone alls to all seven of our children to wish them Merry Christmas. I had started to feel nauseated on our grotto venture and lay down, wondering if I would be able to make the planned Christmas dinner at Gaylord's Restaurant, the former headquarters of a major sugar plantation. Dottie took my temperature and determined I had a bit of a fever, but after an extended siesta I felt I could make it to our reserved dinner.

" The approach to the restaurant was well lighted and at the entrance was a white carriage for rent for those who wished to tour the estate. We learned that Gaylord's was built in 1935, much later than I had imagined. All of the original lovely furnishing in a large living room were on display for viewing by visitors. When we entered the dining area on the lanai, the lead waiter brought Dottie a beautiful orchid lei and said she reminded him of someone beautiful in his past. We speculated that he might be referring to his mother.

"The earlier breeze became a strong wind about the time we were being seated and the menus and place settings were blown off the tables. The many oil burning lamps around the area blew out. Finally the staff lowered plastic and bamboo drapes and we were seated comfortably in their shelter.

"The meal included clam chowder, salmon, turkey and beef, pumpkin pie and a variety of side dishes. They insisted we take the remainders and packed them up fior us, enough for breakfast and lunch the next day, our departure day."

We ate leftovers for breakfast plus an orange for Dottie and an avocado for me. For lunch it was a granola bar for each plus yogurt for Dottie and a leftover Gaylord pork chop for me. In the late afternoon we went through the usual pre-flight hassle, plus a couple of innovations such as "Agricultural Inspection" an event that required all luggage to be unpacked and repacked before we got to the Hawaiian Air counter. There followed much showing of identification and tickets followed by a frisking and shoe removal before proceeding to the gate. The shoe removal at this relatively remote island airport pretty much blew my mind. What would a terrorist be doing on Kauai anyway?

At Honolulu International Airport after our twenty minute flight from Kauai we boarded American Airlines flight 72, departed on time and enjoyed a couple of martinis and a good dinner before settling down for the long flight to O'Hare. On arrival we were informed that out flight to West Palm Beach was overbooked and they would give us five hundred dollars apiece if we would give up our seats and take the next flight. We declined in the interest of getting back to our little nest in Stuart. The final irony was that our flight was delayed and the flight we declined arrived in West Palm Beach well in advance of our arrival. We had turned down a thousand bucks only to arrive later than the alternate flight. Fortunately, our driver was waiting for us as we got off the plane and we were home in an hour and a half, tired but happy we had had our month in another paradise.

WELLS VALLEY DAYS(14)
"There Was an Empty Spot on the Map..."

Breezewood lies near the southern border of Pennsylvania perched on the edge of Sideling Hill Mountain at the junction of Interstate 70, the Pennsylvania Turnpike, US30 and several other roads wandering off into the surrounding hills and mountains. Five miles to the east of Breezewood, near the top of Sideling Hill Mountain, State Road 915 bears off to the left and descends for four miles through a series of heart-stopping ten percent grades and hairpin curves to the valley below. The road had been carved on the rugged mountain through thick woods back before the beginning of the twentieth century, using horse drawn graders, and human operated pick axes. The grades and curves had not been massaged much since that time, although the road has been paved with asphalt. After the four mile descent one can view the vista of Wells Valley, a paradise of forest lands and low hills covered with rolling fields between Sideling Hill Mountain and Broad Top Mountain. There is essentially no level ground; the land in the valley is sloped one way or another.

After another mile on SR915 toward the western end of this valley is the Village of Wells Tannery, the seat of Wells Township, both named for an early arrival in the eighteenth century. Records show that this man for a time operated a small tannery supplied with tannin from the then locally prevalent oak trees. He later left for parts unknown, leaving only his name on the place. This is not exactly a metropolis; there was once a store, but it is long gone and the United States Post Office occupies the decrepit building. The little local store has been superseded by vastly larger stores twenty or thirty miles away, providing an excuse for the local inhabitants to decamp for brighter lights and greater varieties of merchandise in such centers as Bedford to the west and McConnellsburg to the east.

Wells Tannery includes twenty or thirty houses, depending on where you consider the boundaries of the village to be. There are three centers of activity in "the Tannery: the

Post Office, the Wells Valley Presbyterian Church and Wells Valley Township Park.

The United States post office is a ramshackle building which once housed the last remaining store in the village. It occupies the northwest corner of where Cove Road dead ends at Wells Tannery Road, the latter a short loop off State Road 915 that amounts to the main street of Wells Tannery. There is a vacant lot between the post office and the residence of Wells Township Supervisor John Ford behind which the supervisor maintains a group of twenty or so heterogeneous kennels housing an equal number of heterogeneous coon dogs for the frequent occasions when he feels like chasing raccoons around through the valley or down in Virginia where he has access to a few hundred acres, "loaded with 'coons." The supervisor-coon hunter chews tobacco and spits out the juice a few times when describing his coon hunting adventures, conducting his functions as supervisor or passing the time of day with his constituents, often at the post office.

John's devoted wife, Gladys, is a member and mainstay of Wells Valley Presbyterian Church while John would neither join the church nor attend services under any circumstances although the church stands diagonally across the road from the Ford house. Gladys is also a significant participant in the weekly services, leading those in attendance, a group rarely more than fifteen, in singing the customary three hymns, but also rendering a solo in a straining high pitched voice that periodically falters on the high notes.

Wells Valley Park is a short distance to the west, occupying a piece of relatively flat ground at the bottom of the foothills. It is used for the annual Wells Valley Homecoming in July, family reunions, church picnics and occasionally a wedding. There is a baseball diamond, a large food service building and several ancillary shelters used by the country music groups that play for homecoming and other occasions and one for the sale of ice cream by visiting organizations.

It takes a considerable number of volunteers to stage the homecoming; food servers, parking attendants, inside cooks and outside barbecue cooks to broil the five hundred or so chicken halves consumed by the attendees. Many of those who have filled these jobs over many years are getting tired and younger replacements are hard to find because of the lack of opportunity in the area. Nevertheless, Homecoming is an event that attracts hundreds of people from all over western Pennsylvania.

A bit beyond the park on Cove Road, a right of way branches off to the left, where a sign reads, "Koontz Road". Ray Koontz, the fellow who sits next to us in church, married a girl with whom Dottie double dated during those summers when she visited her grandparents in the valley. With the exception of Cove Road, virtually all the roads in the area are named for valley families past or present, i.e. Moseby Road, Koonts Road, Chamberlain Road, Metzier Road, Johnson Lane and so on. Wells Valley Road, as was the valley, were named after the first settler, a man about whom very little is known.

Another surprise to me was the use of the word "cove", which I had always known as a wor describing a sheltering inlet connected to the ocean or a lake. Inland the word is used to describe an area enclosed on three sides by mountains or hills. There are several towns in Western Pennsylvania having names that include the word cove.

Beyond Koontz Road, Cove Road makes a couple of sharp turns and then pretty much peters out as it goes into the Buchanan State Forest, although earlier, in the nineteenth and early twentieth century, it had been the main road to Breezewood. Now it is full of pot holes and barely passable by automobile.

Outside of private transactions, nothing can be purchased commercially in Wells Tannery, except the postage stamps, money orders and other offerings of the post office. The postmaster, a lady named Laurie Baird, doesn't even live in Wells Tannery; she lives in Hollidaysburg, up near Altoona. Her predecessor, Mary Lou Stiffle, didn't live in the valley either; she commuted from Six Springs.

The post office, in addition to its postal functions, serves as a social center for the community, a function that long ago was filled by the now long gone country store. To give a sense of validity to the social aspect of the post office two long benches have been installed, one outside on the sloping porch for use during fair weather days and one inside to be occupied during cold weather or inclement days. Some of the waiting residents carry their morning coffee with them and there also is the basket of candy on the counter, traditionally filled by the postmaster or her assistant, but occasional contributions are also made by the postal customers.

During the months the local gardens are in full production, the post office serves as a distribution point for the excess home gardeners often have. The outside bench provides a place to display zucchini and other squashes, tomatoes, corn and whatever other garden produce is available. All comers are welcome to take what they can use,

The mail is delivered from Altoona by automobile about ten in the morning and then must be sorted to fill the post office boxes assigned to village residents who have chosen to receive their mail that way. The remainder, sorted in order of the rural mail boxes along her delivery route, goes back into the car. Meanwhile the waiting villagers take the opportunity to exchange the local news and gossip and comment on the national news. After the mail is sorted it is quickly retrieved by the waiting group and the morning social hour is over.

The people are getting older in the manner of people everywhere. There is no work other than farming, so the younger people either move away, or they work in towns thirty or more miles away where work is available. "Ain't nothin' ta do here," is a common complaint of the young, while the retirees enjoy their gardening, sewing, whittling and the news and soap operas provided on the cable TV operated by the Booher Brothers over in Waterfall. In the summer time a primary entertainment is sitting on the porch and watching and listening to the roar of the immense trucks on state road 915 hauling trash to fill the abandoned open pit coal mines up toward the Broad Top Mountain.

The farmers primarily grow corn and hay. Starting in early June, the mowers sing a lilting tune from early morning until dark, and, after a short drying period, huge round bales of hay start dotting the hillside fields and are arrayed in rows alongside every road. It's a wonderment how much fuel goes into these efforts, and where the market is for all this hay, but by fall it starts to disappear to markets as far away as Virginia and Maryland.

Hopewell a small town lies to the north and west of Wells Tannery, across the Broad Top Mountain and is the home of a foundry and forge, that produced and repaired the heavy tools needed to extract the coal from the surface mines in the region until the mines closed when production became uneconomical. Now the little building made of rough sawed lumber is a museum displaying the mining tools and other mining equipment of the era all operated by hand as electricity arrived only late in the mining era. Early in our time in Walls Valley we decided to make our way over to Hopewell to visit the foundry museum and visit with friends of Dottie's who owned and operated a small and secluded cattle ranch on the Raystown Branch of the Juniata River.

En route to Hopewell we made a small diversion from the main road to look at a Reformed church that had been established in the late eighteenth century. This little side trip impressed me in several ways; the road to the church crosses over a stream via a covered bridge, the likes of which I had only seen in photographs before and the cemetery adjoining the church containing many hundreds of grave stones, some dating back to the seventeen hundreds.

Dottie's "shack", at the foot of Sidling Hill Mountain, was acquired by her father many years ago as an adjunct to the Kirk properties, which included several hundred acres of mostly wooded land, but also included about thirty acres of tillable field. The house was truly a shack when acquired, having at that time no indoor plumbing, no heating other than kitchen and parlor stoves, and no electricity. Frequent additions and remodelings have made "the shack" a livable, relatively modern abode, overlooking a beautiful meadow lying between two creeks that join just before passing under SR 915 yo form Sidling Hill Creek.

Across Tannery Creek and a small pasture, lies the original Kirk homestead, referred to in family conversations as "the brick house". To Dottie's dismay, the brick house had been sold some years ago, and was in a state of distressing disrepair, after having passed through the hands of several uncaring owners. During one of the periods when we were at the shack the property was up for auction to the highest bidder. The last of those owners were Rocky and Beth Greenland, but Rocky had departed for points unknown and Mrs. Greenland was now living in the house alone. The rumor was that Rocky had said as he left, "Take the damned house, it's yours, I'm going back to Colorado." Rocky left, never to be seen again as far as I know. Beth must have had him sign a quit-claim deed either on that or some previous occasion, because the announcement of the auction only offered the property on a quit claim basis.

For several years Beth had engaged realtors from both Fulton and Bedford Counties and one or two from elsewhere. She had established a price twice what she and her husband had paid for the property and buyers stayed away completely. It was only after that failed effort that auction became her chosen option.

Out of curiosity we walked up the road to where twenty-five or so people were standing waiting for the auction to begin. There were several well-dressed men in suits and ties. There was a couple dressed as the plain people do, and we speculated to ourselves that it would be interesting to have such people as neighbors. The remainder of the gathering were dressed in every day work clothes.

"This will be a silent auction except for my announcing each bid in hundred dollar increments. I will acknowledge the possible closing bids when they occur, and tfinally I will announce the knock down price three times before closing. If you have any questions, now is the time to ask them. The property will be sold on a quit-claim basis. We know of no prior claims against the property."

The bidding began and I attempted to keep track of the nods or fingers that indicated bids. Tim Moseby was standing next to me and I noted he made several beds before stepping back and remarking quietly, "It's not worth it." The plain man made a bid or two and he too stood back. Only the men in city clothes continued the bids until the auctioneer announced the property sold and invited the successful bidder to come into the house for closing. It was later revealed that the new owner of the property was one Tim Wessel from Silver Spring, Maryland, who was reported to be in the gardening and lawn maintenance business.

It was from the vantage point of the shack that Dottie enjoyed extended visits to the valley. It had been her grandparents' home and the venue in which she had enjoyed many happy days in her youth.

RON (15)
"I Done Everything Else and What Not."

Ron Black, our neighbor in Wells Township, although married, lives alone in a well-kept house across State Road 915 from the shack. He is the owner of a large farm across the mountain, the caretaker of Dottie's property, the farmer of some of it, and, finally, our friend and, in time of need, a tremendous help and friend indeed.

Beyond all that, he is one of the most intelligent people we have ever known, and one of the best informed of the general population, whether in Wells Tannery or any where else. His formal education was limited to eight years of attendance at a two-room country school, plus a smattering of secondary education in Florida, Texas and Pennsylvania and, in his words, "My post graduate education came through twenty-five years of hauling heavy and oversize equipment all over the country as a long haul truck driver driving through every state of the lower forty eight except Montana." When I asked him how it happened that he never drove through Montana, his reply was, "Just lucky, I guess."

By drawing room standards, his English is deplorable, filled with double negatives, verb-subject disagreements and incomplete sentences, many of which seem to end in mid-flight as a new subject is introduced. Ron's all-purpose collective noun is, "And what not." Thus a description of what a neighbor in the valley does with his time might be, "He farms a little, baby sits at times for the grand kids, saws some firewood, repairs farm machinery and what not." Our friend's description of how he came into vast store of knowledge is, "The only education I got was in Texas where they have a lot of beautiful cowgirls, horses, pickup trucks and oil wells.

Ron is veritable fountainhead of information and he also has one of the quickest minds I have ever encountered. When I inquired into how he had acquired such a wealth of general information, he said, "Well you can't have driven all over hellandgone like I have, with the radio going all the time, without learning something. I just picked it up here and there, good stuff, bad stuff and what not."

As for quickness of mind, after we returned from Europe following a trip to England and Scotland for a Rotary convention in Glasgow, we posed for him one of the puzzles an English tour guide had posed for the passengers under his tutelage, " God doesn't have one, the queen has very few, but you and I have millions. What is it?" Now all you sophisticates would know the answer to that riddle, but none of us Americanson our bus came up with the solution to that one, even after given several hints by the driver.

It was over a drink on the porch of the shack that we sprang our presumably difficult problem on Ron. We gave him no hints. After dinner Dottie and I played our usual cribbage game and climbed up the stairs to bed. It was about nine. At ten o'clock Ron awakened us by phoning to announce the solution. "An equal," of course, was the answer. It made us feel we had just been a part of a bus load of dummies.

Another time we expressed our curiosity about Joe and Sandy Sharpe, our friends across the road. Dottie had an arrangement with Sandy that the Sharpes and she would "keep an eye" on each others' houses, especially during absences, in an effort of suppress possible looting. Joe had been seriously injured in a trucking accident some years before and had never recovered sufficiently for him to return to work of any kind. That much we had known, but nothing of the details or how the Sharpes managed to live in a beautiful three-bedroom house equipped to house the crippled Joe, his wife and three sons. The sons were away at college, another sizeable financial burden that would be difficult for the average family to carry.

Ron's over the road trucking career had ended when he was involved in an accident which ended his career of driving eighteen wheelers all over the country. After recovery he could at least drive his pickup truck and his tractor, although with considerable pain. After an extended battle with the insurance company or companies involved, they had agreed to comply with the provisions of his personal injury policy and he received a monthly payment, but was required to report yearly for a physical examination by a doctor of the company's choosing.

Joe's case was different from Ron's in one critical way; his employer at the time of the accident was his father-in-law, Raleigh Barnett. It was Raleigh and his wife who provided for Joe's family, and, as Ron was quick to add, Raleigh was financially well able to carry this burden because of his singular success in business. Quite naturally our next question was, "What business was he in?" and Ron's one word answer was "Coal."

Open pit coal mining had been a mainstay of the region for generations, and Raleigh, like so many of the neighbors had worked in and around the mines for his entire adult life, starting out as a scavenger of loose coal while still a boy, working as a miner, and finally as a mine owner when he used some of his meager savings to buy stock in the mine where he worked. Eventually he owned the mine. We would find out more about Raleigh and his career during our further Wells Valley stays.

While Ron was able to live a fairly normal life despite his injuries, Joe was not so lucky. He was confined to the house across the road from the shack virtually all of the time but occasionally mounting his garden tractor for a ride through the spruce trees he had had planted some years earlier, pruning them as he went.

Ron exemplifies "the millionaire next door," and as is typical of such self made men, one would not identify him as such. He is generally quiet of demeanor, dresses most of the time in working clothes, drives a battered pick up truck, pulls his small outboard fishing boat on a trailer that he parks in the back yard of his house, plants and harvests his own crops and doesn't waste a lot of time on trivial things, although he is a fascinating conversationalist and can hold his own in discussions ranging from international affairs to the best mixture of grasses to produce hay for race horses to eat.

He confided to me one time that as a young man he had undertaken the responsibility for caring for his aging parents with the understanding that the farm would be deeded to him eventually and Ron ran the farm as a corn-and-cattle operation for many years. More recently, he sold the farm to a couple from Washington who were anxious buyers for a place to use as a weekend retreat. Although the buyers offered a cash deal, the seller, Ron, insisted they pay only the minimum down and pay the remainder with an interest rate favoring Ron, and with no provision for early payment. Later, making the deal even sweeter, the purchasers built a house in the middle of one of the fields making Ron, as the lien holder, even more secure.

Our next to last summer at the shack ended with the arrival of Hurricane Frances, a storm that was no longer a hurricane as it passed through Maryland and Western Pennsylvania, but which carried with it millions of tons of water which were deposited in that region on a Saturday night. We were well advised in advance of the storm's arrival that precautions should be taken to avoid the threatened flooding as much as possible. We had taken our two cars, a Cadillac and a Mercedes north to the valley for the summer with the intention of leaving one there and flying back and forth between Florida and Pennsylvania on occasion.

The valley had flooded many times before under similar circumstances, and we expected it to do so again. We drove our two cars fairly high up on the side of the hill behind the shack; farther than the water had risen to in the time Dottie and her father had owned the land. Despite this precaution, the waters came up over the electronic "mother boards" of both cars and thus totally destroyed them. As a result, after some wrangling with the insurance company, whose adjustors' offices downstream were also inundated, we received a satisfactory settlement from our insurance companies.

The shack was isolated by the flood, and it was Ron who waded in after the waters had receded somewhat to give us help, and it was he who hitched his tractor to the wooden bridge across the creek and straightened it out so it could be used. The bridge had not washed down the flood by virtue of the fact that Ron, many years before had chained it to a sizable tree next to the creek.

Three cars and a pickup truck were stranded on the little bridge on State Road 915 where it crosses at the junction of the two creeks which join at a point between the meadow and Ron's house. Each had come down the mountain sometime during the night and each driver had mistakenly thought he could make it through the flood only to find himself stalled in the middle of the water flowing over the bridge. Ron had rescued each one in turn and in one case gave the unfortunate victim a pair of his trousers to replace those he somehow had lost as the deluge flowed over his pickup.

Our dilemma was not solved at this point, as we were expected to arrive at a *U.S.S. CASE* ship reunion the following Wednesday. When the power and telephone service were finally restored we got on the phone and the internet only to find that the single used car available within twenty-five miles was a Chevrolet Impala, which we bought on the spot. We really enjoyed that car and drove it for the next year at the end of which we went through one of our periodic and quixotic automobile exchanges described in detail elsewhere in this book.

CHURCH (16)
"Washed in the Blood of the Lamb"

Wells Valley Presbyterian Church is built on the side of the hill that fronts Wells Tannery Road across from the post office in such a way that entry to the sanctuary is either from an outside door accessible only by two long unsheltered sets of concrete steps or from inside the church basement via a set of poorly lighted wooden steps which between levels make a right angle turn through a series of triangular steps, and emerges eventually in the church vestibule. Either of these routes is difficult to navigate, particularly for the elderly or disabled.

Wells Valley Presbyterian Church, the sole survivor of the many small churches that formerly dotted the valley. Some have been razed, some have been remodeled into residences and others stand vacant.

Pete Ford, a church elder and perennial greeter, stands just inside the heavy door and hugs each parishioner as he hands him or her the weekly bulletin. In our case, knowing that Pete and his wife, Pat, usually attend the Sunday dinner at one of the area's fire halls or at the Happy Valley Inn not far from Saxton, we check with him to obtain assurance that we going to attend the right place for dinner after the church service.

The congregation rarely numbers more than twenty five, and we wonder how it can possibly survive financially. For a number of years the pulpit was served by a retired army lieutenant colonel who had been ordained following his military service and joined the community only for the weekend, staying in the pretty little manse over on Moseby Road, but now he had retired again, and the pulpit is filled on Sundays by leaders, some ordained, some not. Those who are ordained are retired and living somewhere within the general area between Bedford and McConnelsburg which includes Wells Tannery. In our opinion, one of the best Sunday leaders was a farmer from across the mountains to the east. He was articulate, down to earth and delivered meaningful well-organized sermons. He usually brought with him his wife and several of the older children of his large family. This enlarged the congregation considerably on those occasions.

Given the fact that the pulpit is filled by an assortment of ordained ministers, lay preachers, and occasionally by members of the congregation, there is usually little or no continuity to the services from week to week. For the same reason, there is often little or no internal rhyme or reason to the sermons.

"Blessed Assurance, page two hundred fifteen in the green hymn book", is announced from the pulpit as the opening hymn for the regular service this July Sunday. There are two different hymn books, one green and one red, so there is always a degree of uncertainty as to which is to be used on any given occasion. Immediately following the announcement from the pulpit, Terry Mallott, the pianist, starts hammering out the chorus of the hymn to set the tone for the congregation, and then launches forthwith into the first stanza before I can find a green hymn book, shuffle my way to page two hundred fifteen and get organized sufficiently to join in singing at a point where the words are "...Spirit, Washed in His Blood..." I'm momentarily distracted by this bloody reference in what my father used to refer to as "the slaughterhouse hymns," but I then carry on bravely.

The names and numbers of the hymns are never printed in the bulletin for good reason; they are selected just prior to the service by the itinerant minister serving for the day, and are announced only as the service progresses. For some time I've been trying to convince Terry that we in the pews need an additional thirty seconds or so to catch up with the action before he launches into the hymn, but he is a person of great exactitude, and it has been difficult to modify this little behavioral matter that leaves me shuffling pages while I should be singing.

Terry plays a key part in the worship service, a role that he fills so proficiently that most of us don't give a great deal of thought to how important it is for him to be present on Sunday morning; or at least we didn't until he was absent one recent Sunday when his job at the Mack Truck plant, forty miles away in Hagerstown, Maryland required his presence. It was comparable to the old adage about never missing the water 'til the well runs dry; we never miss Terry 'til he's not there to provide the music.

The situation might not have been as desperate as in fact it became, had the pulpit been filled with one of the remarkably musical preachers we've had, but in this case the lady minister announced right off that she could not lead the singing due to the loss of a part of her larynx in a bout with cancer, and requested that members of the congregation suggest appropriate hymns to be sung a cappella. When the time came for the first hymn, Elder Dave Smith rose from his seat behind us, and said, "Let's sing Onward Christian Soldiers. Everybody knows it."

Fortunately, the minister said, "First and last verses only."

Everyone knew Onward Christian Soldiers all right, but we all knew it in an assortment of keys. Gladys Ford, who regularly sings a solo at our services, carried the day with the six or eight parishioners on the right side of the church. We on the left joined in an entirely different set of keys, while at the same time, the lively tempo of Onward Christian Soldiers slowed to a dirge. The a cappella cacophony finally, and mercifully, came to an end.

Gladys, ever the faithful soloist when accompanied by Terry, declined to perform a cappella that Sunday. Who could blame her? Occasionally, Gladys presents a reading of a poem, or some brief philosophical prose, but on that fateful day she was not prepared to present such an alternative. The following week, Terry, always cheerful and friendly, was greeted with an enthusiasm even more bountiful than ever.

When Gladys sings, it is truly from her heart, and she puts her all into the performance, as no one else in the tiny congregation either could or would. She strains for the high notes, and the members of the congregation in their seats strain with her. Sometimes she and Terry don't finish at the same time. No matter; it all comes from the heart.

In the vestibule, where Pete Ford stands prior to the service, there is a table covered with religious tracts, get well cards awaiting the signatures of the church goers before sending and other communications of possible interest. There is a rail at the head of the winding stairway coming from the basement, a coat rack and an umbrella stand. Pete greets all arrivals from either direction.

The sanctuary, which is open to the roof, is designed to seat about a hundred, so on any given Sunday most pews are empty. There is a raised area upon which the pulpit is perched. Terry and his piano are to the congregation's left of this stage on the lower level, while to the right on a level with the pulpit is a choir loft with seats for ten. No matter; it is almost never used. Below is the ancient pump organ that served the church well for many years before Terry, not being an organist, began providing the accompaniment for the singing. On the wall behind the pulpit is a huge wooden cross and on the congregational level in front of the pews is a table on which rests a very large Bible flaked by two candelabra. Curious, I checked one Sunday morning and found that the Good Book lies open to the beginning of the New Testament.

On the wall above Terry there is a board on which the previous week's attendance and collection are displayed. On one representative week the board displayed the number twenty-six for attendance and $122.60 for the collection.

As we climbed out of our car in front of the church one morning, Bill Moseby, standing at the foot of the stairs leading up to the church entrance, was so deeply engaged in a serious conversation with Steve Knepper, another church elder, that I poked him gently with my cane asking, in effect, that they give us access to the steps. Bill and Steve were still talking seriously when I glanced back from the top of the second long set of steps. I concluded to myself that there was some weighty church-related matter occupying their discussion.

Bill hardly waited for his wife, Carolyn, to be seated, when he rushed to the front of the church and leaned down next to Terry, seated on the piano bench. A serious discussion ensued, but they spoke in hushed tones, and I couldn't get the gist of what the emergency was even though we were seated in our usual place in the front row of pews not more than ten feet from where Terry was sitting at the piano,

I concluded, as it appeared to me, that three church stalwarts were conferring on some matter of considerable importance. Could it be that the termites had finally eaten through the timbers supporting the church? Was the new elevator malfunctioning? Rape? Infidelity? Incest? Bill finally took his seat, and the service began.

I could hardly wait until the itinerant preacher had delivered the benediction at the end of the service, when I would be able to ask what all the discussion was about. Terry always stops to greet us as he turns from the piano and heads for the back of the sanctuary, so I asked as he grasped my hand, "What was all that discussion about? Is there some kind of trouble in the church or community?"

Terry laughed."Oh, no. Bill's just having trouble adjusting the hydraulic clutch on his tractor and he wanted to make sure he knew how to fix the problem. Part of my job is to adjust those things all the time, and Bill just wanted my input. He wasn't sure Steve knew what he was talking about." I was greatly relieved that the perceived emergency had passed.

Inside the church, to the left front of the sanctuary is a door that provides an exit to the sloping ground outside, perhaps valuable as a fire escape, but otherwise not readily usable for ingress or egress, since to enter it, one would have either to climb the hill or descend from above on the grassy slope. It's not clear why the church was built on this site and in this manner, rather than across the road, where level access to the sanctuary would have been available. The members must have been relatively young and spry then.

Several years ago, recognizing that the small congregation was largely elderly, the consistory determined to provide better access, particularly for elderly people. Although Dottie and I are only in the community for a few weeks in the summer, and thus not regular members of the congregation, as I listened to the discussions of the problem for several summers past, I reflected to myself, and possibly suggested to one or two others, that either the upper story of the church, containing the sanctuary, should be moved across the road to a relatively level location, or that a new church be built across the road and the old church be sold to be remodeled and used for some other purpose, perhaps a dwelling, as had been done with several other valley churches.

If any such thoughts were considered, they were quickly rejected and a decision was made to procure an elevator, the installation of which required a small addition to the church building. Three of the elderly members of the congregation promptly died, one moved away to be with a son in the far west, and one retired to an assisted living facility in McConnelburg, so the elevator at present is normally used only by the two remaining truly elderly parishioners. It is apparent, however, when one surveys the little group of church goers that assembles after struggling up one or the other of the stairs leading to the sanctuary on Sunday morning, that others will soon be availing themselves of this vertical transportation.

The sermons are frequently masterpieces of tangled syntax, for example, "We extend our Christian sympathy to Mrs Smith on the death of her husband who died last week of cancer and her friends." Conflicting references in sermons are common. One preacher in a single prayer referred to "World without end," in one paragraph of his entreaty and in another "Until the end of time." I maintain my right to be confused, "Does time end or not?"

Following the service we were always ready to follow Pete's lead for an abundant Sunday dinner at one of the fire halls close enough for an easy commute, Six Mile Run, Robertsdale and Saxton. For four dollars apiece, we each we could stuff ourselves with plain but delicious food and listen to the local news offered by those seated around us. Church, fires and fire hall activities, crops, animals, fishing, hunting, auctions and the accomplishments of children, now mostly grown and thriving in other areas were the principal topics. National politics rarely entered the mix of subjects. On the fourth Sunday of the month there was no fire hall offering so to fill the gap we would go to Happy Hollow a unique restaurant about five miles north of Saxton. The proprietor was an ancient man who stoutly professed that he opened the establishment strictly as a service to the community, The menu was far broader then at the fire halls, and only slightly more expensive. The owner seemed to be always present, but he was never seen to do anything other than making the rounds and chatting with the diners, occasionally taking a seat at a table, apparently when the topic was too heavy or too extensive for him to remain on his feet.

AUCTIONS (17)
"Yer Already in fer a Dollar...".

Harold Baumgardner, was, in a sense, "the squire of Wells Tannery." He had inherited the image, if not the active role, from his father and grandfather, both of whom had truly been "leaders and shakers" of the small community from the early or mid-nineteenth century. They had run the general store in the building diagonally across from the Wells Tannery Post Office.

The Harold I knew for a few years was far from being a mover and shaker; he was more similar to Mr. Milquetoast. He had been drafted into the army in the middle of World War II, and found himself in one of the half-trained divisions held in reserve prior to the time of the Battle of the Bulge. His division, along with several others, was overrun by the German blitz, and Harold became a German prisoner. The war in Europe ended five months later. Harold was physically uninjured, but the experience evidently had a profound influence on him.

It was said that he was married once for about three days. Evidently, married life was not for him. He inherited a beautiful four bedroom stone-faced house from his parents. It had every modern convenience. After the death of his parents, he lived there alone until his death in 2004. Harold's younger brother, Bill, was said to be far more outgoing, but was killed in the crash of his private plane. Harold would never fly, even in a commercial airliner; he might suffer a similar fate.

Bill left two children, Harold's niece and nephew, but as far as anyone in the valley knew, they never visited or otherwise paid any attention to Uncle Harold. Although he never held a job, Harold took care of his own affairs until late in life, at which time he was helped in both personal and financial affairs by members of the small Wells Valley Presbyterian Church congregation of which he was a member.

Harold bounced in and out of Veterans' hospitals until his death. He would daringly enter the elevator in the VA hospital, but when the Wells Valley Presbyterian Church installed an elevator to accommodate people of his generation, he refused to ride in it.

Finally, when the physicians at the VA hospital announced that Harold was on his death bed, his only living relatives, in a sudden burst of concern, expressed great interest in his condition. As his sole heirs, they didn't have long to wait.

Upon his death they arrived promptly to sort out the antiques and other possessions they wanted for themselves, listed the house for sale and arranged for an auction to be held shortly thereafter. The heirs threw out a large quantity of things deemed not worthy of auction, but many of those items were saved when neighbors, arriving before the weekly trash collection, sorted though the "trash" and hauled away treasures.

Despite these inroads into the total accumulation of three generations, a large quantity and variety of goods remained. Several days before the scheduled auction, an immense tent, easily capable of sheltering several hundred people was set up on the lawn directly in front of the house. It would protect prospective bidders, the curious and those seeking only entertainment, from either sun or rain

Curious myself, I dropped by on Friday, the day before the scheduled late August auction. In the garage, among a collection of hundreds of assorted items, lay a beautiful mahogany ship's wheel. I needed no further motivation to attend the auction; the sight of that gorgeous piece of wood work clinched it. I would certainly be a bidder on it. If I could bid it in, it would make an impressive display under Mary Porter's watercolor of Lorelei on the wall of our new apartment in Florida!

What was Harold doing with a ship's wheel in land-locked Wells Valley? One could hardly guess. Harold had never in his life seen any broad water except when he was given a free round trip to Europe in 1944-5, as a guest of Uncle Sam's army.

Further inspection revealed a toolbox containing four jack knives, a bunch of good wrenches, drill bits and other goodies. If I could buy it, the stool in the kitchen could ease the strain on my back when cooking. I couldn't wait for Saturday, the morning of the auction.

We rose early so I could get to the scene for more of a look. The auction was scheduled for nine o'clock, but when I arrived at eight, the house and grounds were swarming with people. Two food trucks were set up in the driveway, and dozens of valley folks were munching on sweet rolls and drinking coffee as they wandered in and out of the house and garage looking over the goods for sale.

The auctioneer was Lyle Reed, a tobacco chewing motor mouth from McConnellsburg. He and his team had all the furniture and other large items numbered and listed on sheets in the order in which they would be sold. Two women in a specially-equipped mobile office, a small house trailer, registered prospective bidders and assigned to each a number which appeared on both sides of a paddle similar to a ping pong paddle. The numbers of winning bidders would be recorded for each item sold. Although a relative late-comer, I received the number twenty-eight when I registered, but I soon realized some early arrivals had registration numbers in the hundreds and concluded that the numbers were randomly issued.

At eight fifty-five the auctioneer announced, "At nine o'clock we're gonna sell the items in the garage, so if yer interested, gather 'round," after which he reached into his shirt and pulled out a package of Plough Boy chewing tobacco and stuffed an impressive amount of the stuff into the left side of his mouth. I set my chair down in front of the garage door and sat down. Promptly at nine, the major domo mounted a little portable stand that elevated him a head or so above the crowd. His daughter was a member of his team and accompanied him to record the bids. "Now we have here this heavy duty shop vise that's worth at least a hunnert dollars; let's start..at-tat..tat-seveny-five-t'-t'-fifty, who'll give tweny-five? t'..t'...twenty..who'll gimmee ten....?" The staccato rattle of an expert auctioneer filled the air with sounds and a tempo that cannot be portrayed in print. The auction was underway.

Luggers from Auctioneer Reed's team dragged things out of the garage as fast as they could be sold: crow bars and pitch forks; axes and sledge hammers; garden hose and a fifty-foot length of two-inch rope were sold, "all to go"; a chain hoist, hand tools and a two-man cross-cut saw; a lawnmower and then a box nails, bolts, screws and miscellaneous hardware, once again, all to go.

Kids were running all over the place, but one little toddler, not more than three, insisted on standing on his wobbly legs about four feet in front of where the luggers displayed the wares, often swinging an axe, a pitchfork or other dangerous tool for attention. I thought the little guy would be beheaded, or at least seriously injured at any minute, but no mother arrived to protect or remove him. I leaned toward the elderly overall-clad man next to me and said, "Why doesn't somebody pull the kid out of that dangerous situation?"

He said, "I dunno. Seems like people our age are the only ones who worry about kids these days. If you want to see his Mom, just reach out there and try to pull him away. She'll be here right fast. "

I bid in the toolbox containing the knives, wrenches, drill bits and a bunch of other junk for five bucks. Shortly thereafter a lugger picked up the coveted ship's wheel. My heart skipped a beat and then accelerated in tempo. The auctioneer started his rattling lingo and two minutes later, success. I was the proud possessor of the beautiful mahogany piece and seventy-five dollars poorer. In ten minutes the garage was emptied.

The auctioneer then moved his headquarters to the enormous tent, where he mounted a dais supporting a gray pulpit adorned with a large red "L/R" logo for Lyle Reed. The recorder was at his side. I moved my lawn chair to a position in the front row. The staccato chant resumed. Fingers, nods and the numbered cards signified bids, coming now at a breakneck pace. Pillows, sheets, tableware, bedspreads, glassware, Persian rugs, clocks, lamps and kitchen ware were knocked down apace, all interspersed with "box lots" containing miscellaneous stuff of astonishing variety. These offerings gave rise to much country humor and bantering.

Occasionally the audience seemed to have no interest. Along with a couple of others, I started opening the bidding with one finger, a move appreciated by the auctioneer. This usually started the process and someone else would later bid in the item. Two times, however, my bid was "in for one dollar." On the first occasion I came into possession of a box containing a bed pan, a beautiful little tea pot and a bunch of worthless trinkets. My other one dollar bid brought me a three piece set of Samsonite luggage which apparently had never been used – a tremendous bargain! Five minutes later a steamer trunk from a long gone era brought several hundred dollars.

Furnishings were alternated with box goods and individual items in the procession of things that came across the front of the assembled bidders, gawkers and curious. A guy who looked more like a real Santa Claus than many of the department store variety had been wandering around the place, apparently with a specialized interest. He wore a khaki outfit with his pants tucked into rubber boots. His beard hung down to the middle of his chest, and his flowing gray hair reached the middle of his back. When a shabby-looking Persian rug was held up, he bid it in for four hundred dollars. Later in the sale other rugs brought similar prices from him. He bought an ancient desk, said to have been used in the Baumgardner store, for five hundred dollars. The purchaser of these valuable item was an antique dealer, and knew what he was doing. Later, as I waited in line behind him to pay for my few things, Santa Claus peeled hundred dollar bills from a wad he withdrew from a leather pouch chained to his belt to pay up an account of several thousand dollars.

At one point the auctioneer paused from his seemingly endless chatter to take a drink from the glass on his pulpit, and a man in the crowd yelled, "Lyle, you should be a preacher."

The agile-tongued auctioneer shot back, "I am a preacher. I've gotta preach in four different churches tomorrow, McConnellsburg Church of the Brethern, Pine Grove Methodist, Wells Valley Presbyterian and The Orbisonia Church of What's Happenin' Now! I'll be pooped by the end of the day." With that he turned toward the house in back of him and let go a stream of tobacco juice into the hedge. The bidding resumed.

By ten thirty, the lunch wagon was doing a land office business. It looked as though half the crowd was munching on hamburgers, hot dogs, French fries or candy bars. The other half was sucking up Pepsi, coffee or Mountain Dew. Some of the older kids were throwing a football around in back of the office trailer. Others were swinging from the branches of a willow tree. The rattling staccato of the auctioneer pervaded the atmosphere. When I checked the Porta-Pottie in the back yard, there was a line of six women waiting for its use. I relieved myself, country style, against a tree behind the hedge that delineated the yard from the surrounding farm land.

Back at the scene of action, I once again raised a finger to indicate a starting bid on a box of "junk". Lyle's droning tones continued, and I was distracted for a moment as I stepped up to the table to see what was actually in the box. There was a set of six cut glass tumblers among the other stuff. I thought it worthy of another bid. I sat down and put my finger back in the air to indicate a bid. Not missing a beat, the auctioneer announced, "Heyell, Fritz, yer already in fer a dollar. Sold, number twenty-eight fer one dollar."

Heavy black clouds were rolling across the western sky as the noon hour approached. An ancient dining room table and six ladder-back chairs went for almost a thousand dollars. The eating and bidding continued, but some folks, satisfied with their new possessions, started to load their cars, SUV's and pickup trucks, looking up at times to check the oncoming storm.

Lyle stopped his chatter for a moment, took a sip of water and shot another four-inch stream of tobacco juice into the hedge. "We'll be all done here by twelve fifteen," he announced. The last item, another old steamer trunk in perfect condition, brought four hundred dollars. "That's it folks. Thanks for coming. Drive safely and don't get wet....Looks like it'll be rainin' in another ten minutes." Vehicles were departing the scene in droves. I loaded up my treasures and brought them to the shack for Dottie's inspection. It had been a great day.

In another year during our winter absence we received word from Wells Tannery that Mary Horton had died in a nursing facility in McConnellsburg. It was Mary who brought flowers from her beautiful garden every summer Sunday and for many years she played the wheezing old pump organ during church services, but as her arthritis worsened she asked to be relieved of this duty and she was replaced by Terry Mallott who played the piano.

Mary had lived alone in the immense family house diagonally across the road from the church for many years after the departure of her several children and the death of her husband, but now, with no family members remaining in Wells Tannery the family decided it was time to dispose of the surplus of things remaining in the house beyond those that were keepsakes selected for the surviving family members.

On our daily visit to the Post Office, Dottie and I noted the considerable activity at the Horton house so we stopped on our way home hoping to have a preview of the things to be sold. Initially we were shied away by a lady who had come out of the house to the porch to shake out a rug, but when Dottie spoke she was recognized as an old friend and we were invited to tour the house and view the contents. Once again, as with Harold Baumagdner's house, I was amazed with not only the quantity of things to be sold, but also the great variation in the quality of what was to be offered; there was everything from fruit jars and toys to valuable pieces of furniture. I noted that there were many hand woven rugs and quilts of the kind that had been sold at the previous auction for hundreds of dollars apiece.

Dottie took an interest in several dolls, some without certain body parts like arms and legs but finally set her eyes on a tinplate Ferris Wheel and indicated she would like to buy it. Her friend, who turned out to be one of the Horton daughters said, "The auctioneer has asked us not to allow any pickers in the house as they are seeking to buy selected items at prices lower than they can get in an antique store, or on the general market. Come back tomorrow and bid on the Ferris Wheel. It probably won't bring much. The spring is broken."

Auction day found us seated on the low stone wall that seemed to mark the boundary between the front and back yards of the Horton house. On the porch and on the lawn in front of us were hundreds of items, many in boxes and baskets. We knew from our visit that numerous other items, including furniture were still in the house. Dottie spotted the Ferris Wheel somewhere in the well organized clutter and remarked again that she'd like to buy it.

A rather handsome man wearing a suit and a tie approached and inquired, "Do you mind if I join you here on the wall?" We nodded assent, he took his place next to Dottie and we opened a discussion that included a comment from Dottie that she would like to bid on the Ferris Wheel, but really didn't know what would be an appropriate price to pay for it. Further conversation revealed that our new friend was a picker and that he owned an antique shop in Bedford.

"What do you think that Ferris Wheel will go for?" Dottie finally asked.

"Oh, anywhere from fifty to a hundred dollars," he replied, There are collectors around who might pay more than that." I tried to intervene with a comment that the spring on the tinplate.

Presently the auctioneer stood on an old apple crate and announced, "The auction will start in five minutes, so if you don't have a paddle, go on over to my trailer parked yonder and get yourself one. No bids without a paddle." Our picker had already signed up for what looked like a ping pong paddle with fifty four in large numbers on either side. I had seen a couple of items on which I thought I'd bid, including a couple of tools and an old sixteen gauge shotgun, so I strode over as the bidding began and signed up for a paddle.

The auctioneer was droning, "And now, foks, we have this beautiful percolator coffee maker. Let's start the bidding at ten dollars. Who'll give me ten dollars? Seven fifty?...Who'll give me a bid?" An older man wearing bib overalls raised one finger and the bidding began. There were a few desultory buds shortly thereafter and then, preceded by the customary "Going once, going twice, going three times," he announced, "Sold to the lady in the pretty pink dress." I found myself thinking that this guy was going to be all right, but he certainly was no match for Lyle Reed, notably in regard to entertaining his audience.

After an hour or so an assistant fetched the Ferris Wheel and handed it to the auctioneer. "Now here is a splendid example of tin plate art that the Horton kids grew up with and maybe some of you Wells Tannery neighbors played with it, too. The spring is busted, but so what? I've seen ones just like it down to the antique stores for a hundred and fifty bucks." The guy knew his lines, all right.

I winced when Dottie took me by the arm and asked, "Will you bid on it for me?"

I replied, "Honey, I don't know much about that kind of stuff, but it looks like a piece of junk to me."

She turned to the man next to her and inquired, "Will you bid on it for me?"

He said, I'll be glad to. What's your upper limit?"

Based on what she had been told earlier, she said, "Fifty dollars." I winced and looked the other way down toward the trailer. The bidding went rapidly through the lower numbers and finally with a raised finger our friend bought the old rusted Ferris Wheel for fifty dollars, but not for his own account; the Ferris Wheel was Dottie's. She dutifully paid him the fifty dollars and he was kind enough to waive any fee that might have been due for his services.

An hour later, sitting there on the bench, Dottie began having second thoughts. She poked the man next to her and said, "You told me this Ferris Wheel was well worth fifty dollars and now I'm no longer certain I want it. Will you give me fifty dollars for it?"

"Oh no," the man replied, "I wouldn't pay more than twenty-five fore it. My business is to sell for a profit, and that means I have to make at least a hundred percent of my purchase price. But you'll have no problem, put is up for sale in either Bedford or McConnelburg and you'll get more than your money back." He turned his attention to the quilts and paid several hundred dollars apiece for two of them. Two of the other particularly fancy quilts purchased by others went for prices above seven hundred dollars each.

I was very impressed with the prices paid for these hand quilted treasurers, but I was even more impressed later when the quilting frame on which they all had been produced was purchased for ten dollars. Apparently no one in our ever more pressured society still had either the time or the inclination to produce such treasures themselves.

Several days later Dottie was certain she now longer wanted the rusty old Ferris Wheel. There were several reasons for us to go to McConnelsburg and one of them was to be shed of the erstwhile treasure. At the antique store on Main Street, the proprietor looked the toy over carefully, spun its wheel a few times and announced, "I think it will bring about three hundred dollars. I'll take it on commission and when it sells we'll split the profit." He wrote a receipt on a pad preprinted for that purpose and handed it to her. Many events in our lives overrode the relatively unimportant matter of the Ferris Wheel and we have neither heard from the antique dealer nor attempted to contact him. Perhaps the toy is still being viewed in the window of the McConnelburg antique store.

COSTA RICA (18)

An Adventure Between Two Oceans

"Where shall be go this year? How could any venture be better than our five weeks in Hawaii?" The discussion had barely begun when we said simultaneously, "Somewhere in Latin America; neither of us has ever been there." It didn't take long for us to settle on Costa Rica, a Central America country with a reputation for cordiality, and one that had been at peace with itself since shortly after World War II; it had suffered no recent revolutions.

Equipped now with a laptop computer, we wrote extensive descriptions of our activities during our six weeks in the country. The following is an abridged version of our adventures in beautiful Costa Rica:

Our preparations consisted of pacjing our bags and making two reservations through our affiliation with an inexpensive military reservation system that disposes of unused time share periods. On the appointed day after aride to the airport with our friendly driver. our passports were checked before boarding, and a little more than three hours later, when we disembarked in San Jose, Costa Rica's capital, our life became considerably more exciting. After a lengthy entry process, we were allowed to proceed to baggage claim, and after another wait, our baggage appeared, and with that we alternated bathroom calls, having been warned repeatedly, that one of us had to stay to watch over our things. We finally got to place our bags, our refrigerated medications (so we thought), our lap-top, and incidentals on a conveyor belt to pass through visual scrutiny and then another pass through what appeared to be an X-ray device.

When we loaded our bags onto our cart as they came out of this device, our carry-on bag with all of our meds was not there. Terror struck! We tried to speak to anyone and everyone who appeared to be in authority. None knew a word of English, and, in our panic, our limited Spanish escaped us entirely. It appeared to us that some other passenger, long gone, had picked up our meds by mistake. Long lines of departing passengers continued to stride past us with their baggage under control. What were we to do? Neither of us could survive very long without our meds. We continued attempting to describe our anguish to sympathetic but seemingly uncomprehending attendants.

Finally, with much arm-waving, and many smiles, we were beckoned to follow a gun-toting guard, who, after having us describe the bag about a dozen times with hand gestures, led us to a smiling young lady, who demonstrated. also by gestures, where we had managed to drop the bag from our cart without noticing. She then led us to a pile of assorted pieces of baggage that others had misplaced and proceeded to hand us our bag of medicines. Enormous relief!

We headed for the EuroCar rental booth; it was two in the afternoon, the time at which we had indicated we would pick up the car. After a lengthy discussion, and several phone calls by the agent concerning insurance, we were allowed to load our baggage and sign off for the car's condition. Dottie got into the passenger seat and we were turned loose. I had never before driven a vehicle with the driver's seat on the right, but off we went, not really knowing fully where the five speeds forward or the reverse were on the stick shift.

Down the Pan American Highway we went in unbelievably heavy traffic for a Sunday afternoon. We had been instructed that to get to Villas Palmas, where we had reserved a villa, we should first get to the Hotel Irazu, (A Best Western) by making two 360-degree turns, both clockwise, after exiting the highway. After having done this three full times without success, and managing to get back onto the highway west bound each time through a traffic-laden "round-about", we decided to take the *second* right-hand exit after the first 360-degree turn. Success! We finally made it to Villas Palmas, and at our hail, the gate was opened, and were welcomed. We were happy, but exhausted.

Our apartment far exceeded both our needs and expectations. On the first floor were a sitting room, dining room, bedroom, half bath and fully-equipped kitchen. On the second floor were two bedrooms, a sitting area and two full baths. There were televisions in both living rooms. We were living in the lap of luxury, with sleeping space for four couples! Perhaps this spoiled us a bit for what was yet to come. We were happy to flop into bed at the end of this extended and tiring day.

We were greeted on Monday morning in the Villas Palmas courtyard with bright sunshine and a complimentary breakfast, accompanied with pitches by Mark Ayala, a tour operator headquartered nearby. The rice was heavily laden with "*salsa ligano*", essentially, we were told, the national spice of Costa Rica. We can eat it, but don't really like it.

Our first stop was at a branch bank at the Irazu to buy *colones,* the Costa Rican currency. They rejected my VISA card, and Dottie had left hers in her purse back in our quarters, so we perforce returned to retrieve it. We didn't attempt any further adventuring that day.

One of the most surprising and frustrating things about Costa Rica is the complete absence of street signs and house numbers. There are signs giving general directions to cities and towns and to named communities within them, but beyond that, nothing. With the exception of central San Jose, although streets are named, the names are not used on the maps. In central San Jose, the north-south streets and the east-west avenues are named on the map, but there are no signs along the streets themselves. All directions are given by naming landmarks, i.e., "*dereche de* MacDonald's" or *pasado el cathedral*", etc., accompanied by much waving of arms. All Catholic churches are built facing west, and that fact helps somewhat in maintaining orientation. The total of these observations helps to explain why the mail system is largely ineffective. Unless one has a post office box, an "*apartado*", there is no way for the system to get mail to the addressee.

We were counseled to take a taxi when going into the city, as the traffic in and around San Jose is nothing less than intimidating, with three vehicles squeezed into the lanes for two. Bicycles and motor bikes scoot in between and around all other vehicular traffic. Horns are blowing constantly, and cars often have no more room between them than a coat of paint. Public transportation in the form of taxis and busses, all painted red, add to the press. For the most part, the busses are repainted U.S. school busses; some with the tops removed at the seat level. Although we didn't try it, we were told several times that one can board a bus at any point in the country and, with enough transfers, get to any other bus stop. Attempts to maintain railroads in Costa Rica have long since been abandoned, as it is impossible to maintain rail alignment in a country where the earth is constantly shifting due to volcanic action.

We made several expeditions into the central city, toured the National Theater, the cathedral the central park and the Grand Hotel, all impressive buildings. We determined to attend a Rotary meeting, and after a jolting ride over pot-hole ridden streets, we were dropped off in front of Club Union in downtown San Jose. The luxurious and exclusive Club Union is where the elite meet, and the San Jose Rotary club, founded in 1927, meets there most of the time, but every fourth week it meets elsewhere, often in a member's private home in the evening, and spouses are invited to attend.

I had done a bit of agonizing over whether I should wear a jacket. Fortunately, jacket and tie won out, for as soon as we entered the building we noted that all men were wearing dark suits and ties. All service personnel were immaculately uniformed. As we were early, we went across the street to *Banco Seguiridad* to acquire some colones using now our VISA card successfully. While Dottie made the exchange, I went to the men's room and donned my jacket and tie.

The Club Union is a beautiful building with floors which are alternately marble and inlaid tropical woods. Many of the walls are of mahogany as well. The foyer features a statue of Mercury and a spectacular spiral staircase, which ascends to both the second and third floors of the club. A stunning three-story crystal chandelier hangs through the core of the spiral. The circular portion of the third floor ceiling from which the chandelier hangs is patterned glass mirror inlayed with gold to complete the design. When we were in the foyer, both on arrival and departure, we could hear piano music emanating from one of the two first-floor bars.

A staff member escorted us to the elevator, no doubt recognizing that climbing the stairs would be quite an effort for us. When we entered the second floor foyer, we were greeted with typical Rotary cordiality, and were soon being escorted by a newly-found German émigré friend, Vincent Schmack, who speaks very good English. The meeting was conventional Rotary, opening with an invocation The meal was served by formally dressed staff with entrees of both chicken and pork. Salad, rice, fruit and a choice of desserts completed the menu. Dottie was particularly impressed by the chairs on which we all sat. They were completely enclosed by white linen covers designed so they could easily be removed for laundering at frequent intervals a hygienic feature of which my nurse wife heartily approved.

The program included a review of the objects of Rotary and recitation of the Four-Way Test. A highlight was the induction of a new third generation member by his grandfather, a long-time Rotarian.

As we departed, I struggled with at least some success to get a digital picture of the beautiful spiral staircase, the statue of Mercury, the chandelier, Christmas tree and other Christmas decorations. On our return to our quarters, Mark had received directions to the BIRD HOUSE, an establishment in the northern mountains suggested by Mark.

With that, we decided to venture a drive to Cartego which turned out to be a further exposure to some of the hair-raising aspects of driving in Costa Rica. We were well briefed on how to get onto the by-pass around central San Jose, so we managed that with no problem. To get to the turn off from the by-pass and onto the road toward Cartago required that we go through four "roundabouts", each of which was an adventure in itself with only inches between the cars competing for the lanes. We visited the ruins of a never completed cathedral, ate a lunch of fruit and were successful in transiting the rounabouts on our return to San Jose.

Eventually our time in San Jose was over, so once again we drove down Highway #2 toward Cartago. We made all the turns properly until we got to the three-way separation just before Cartago, where we took the wrong one, wound up driving through a myriad of dirt roads trying to find our way and finally, after a great deal of agony got back onto a paved road and managed to return to Cartago

Back in Cartago, we tried without initial success to get directions from a friendly group of men conversing on the walkway at the side of the street. One of the men seated on the front step of a house hailed another person through the open door of the house. The responder to this summons was a gentleman who forthwith offered to lead us in his car back to Highway #2. We followed our new-found friend on a harried drive back to the confusing three-way intersection. Our friend stopped, and we thanked him as effusively as we knew how. He absolutely refused to take payment of any kind; another example of the generally kindly and gentle nature of the *Ticos*. He pointed down the road and said it would be two hours to San Isidro du General. We were on our way!

The road started to rise almost immediately, and we spent most of the next two hours climbing through the mountains in intense, thick, overwhelming rain forest. Round large leaves and hanging plant fronds were all around us. There were sharp turns and steep grades, leading me to remark, "I find myself chewing on my heart much of the time!" Actually the roads are similar to two-lane mountain roads in the United States. The only real problems were the numerous unfilled pot-holes.

Right on the dot of two hours elapsed time, we broke out into a valley and shortly were in the town of San Isidro. Our

Fodor's had said that our hotel was six kilometers south of the city on the highway. Naturally, we doubted whether we were on the right road, so we resolved if we didn't find it by seven kilos, we would have to start asking and "group groping". When we had gone about six kilometers, we saw a taxi standing next to the road, so we pulled up next to the driver and asked, "*Donde' esta el Hotel del Sur?*" He pointed across the road and said, "*Entrado el amarillo driveway*" We were there!

The desk clerk helped us unload our gear, and get us established. We found ourselves in a very nice room with bath, but there were no cooking facilities. I won the first cribbage game there and we then proceeded to the dining room where Dottie ordered spaghetti with beef in the restaurant with a salad; I had the fried fish with veggies, both very good.

Monday morning, we ate the *Tico* breakfast including eggs *ligano* salsa, rice and beans, and then set out to explore San Isidro, starting at the church and the town square. There was some kind of festival or celebration going on with people, people people everywhere! The square has numerous benches, which we used on occasion as we explored. There was a small tilt-a-wheel, a merry-go-round and a couple of other mini-rides. There were large piles of food on a mobile serving trailer, and we took a picture. Later, we sought to have a chocolate ice cream cone, but wound up with some sweet ice speckled with bits of colored gelatin. When we got tired, we went home and took a pre-dinner nap.

We treated ourselves to a delicious filet mignon for dinner at the hotel restaurant and then went to the little casino, and played the slots with Costa Rican coins worth about twenty-five cents each. Early on, I hit three 7's, for c/7400, so we quit and went to bed, ahead by about twenty dollars. (The exchange rate at the time was about 370/1.)

We determined to drive over to the Pacific Ocean toward a place identified as Dominical. In downtown San Isidro, the sign on the highway at the church indicated a left turn to Dominical. That led us past the park, up the mountainside, to a dead end, with a choice of left or right. Each direction led to another dead end, so back to the square we went.

We inquired of a taxi driver, and he waved us to another left turn at the end of the park. There was no sign or any other indication that this might be the way to Dominical. The route led us through the suburbs, past an agricultural co-op, and then up the steep twisting turns we were becoming accustomed to. All the while climbing, we passed occasional little settlements, churches, stores and farms. We drove most of this in the third of the four gears but occasionally in second.

At last it appeared we were at the top, and we coasted on down along a twisting stream bed toward the Pacific. At the bottom we hit a smooth four-lane unmarked road and finally found Dominical. There was nothing there but a muddy, unpaved street, a few houses and a *super Mercado* with floor space of about eight by twelve feet.

With that, it was back up over the mountain for the thirty four kilometers to home. The next day we drove up the side of Mount Iruzu until the road ended and the hiking trail began. Hiking up a mountain was not for us in our eighties!

Thursday was to be our last full day at Hotel del Sur, so we determined to head out for the border with Panama about two hundred kilometers to the southwest. The Pan American highway south is mostly through rolling agricultural country, and was easy driving. We noted that while there were many beef cattle, horses and chickens there were no hogs visible; dogs are ubiquitous. We passed many hundreds, or perhaps thousands, of acres of pineapple fields, and also a Del Monte canning factory.

After much driving, we rolled into the border town of Canoes. What a change from the countryside we had been traveling! People, cars and trucks were scurrying in every direction. Little boys were both beckoning and trying to give us directions. There was much shouting and honking of horns. The road narrowed to a single lane, with traffic going both ways, and with stores as well as open markets on either side of the road.

Street vendors were everywhere, some on tricycles, strenuously hawking their wares. Although we had wanted to see the actual border, we decided that this was close enough. We took a detour into a side street and made a procedure turn for home. We did manage to take a couple of pictures while engaged in this somewhat stressful traffic situation.

Regrettably, we did not take a picture of the cute little girl holding in each hand a coconut with a sipping straw sticking out from one of its eyes, Afterward, I said, "We should have bought a couple of those coconuts."

Two towns back up the road in Chacarita, we stopped for lunch. No one spoke a single word of English...*nada*...so we pointed our fingers on menu items and settled for *pollo fritos, arrozzo, salade con tomat y muchos ligano*. We liked it despite the *ligano*. We stopped briefly at one of the thousands of hectares of fields full of carefully cultivated plants to verify those were actually pineapples growing there, and I won my little bet with Dottie, who sometimes is hard to convince.

On Friday the thirteenth, we were up and bathed early. Finally, we were checked out and on our way to Jaco. It was nine o'clock.

And now it was to be back up over the mountain range to Dominical, thence onward to Quepos and Jaco. For example, on one occasion a sign read, "Dominical 10 Kilometers," and then after driving about five kilometers, another sign read, "Dominical 10 Kilometers!" I remarked to Dottie, "Dominical is moving as fast as we are."

As predicated by Fodor, the road from Dominical to Quepos is, at best, washboard gravel. Read: "Rough rock-laden road." It was a joint-jarring, rib-rattling, bone-busting ride on which the only smooth parts were when traversing the numerous single lane steel plate or wooden bridges. Traffic from one direction or the other is required to stop for as long as it takes for the oncoming traffic to pass, whether one or a dozen vehicles. This requirement is indicated by an *Alto* sign on the obligated side of the bridge. Many bridges do not have side rails and the wheels of the car are seemingly at the edge of the bridge on either side. These bridges gave our bones brief moments of respite from the jarring experience on the rest of the road.

Fortunately, the route is essentially flat, running along the Pacific coast, a kilometer or so inland. We soon realized that the major crop of the region is the oil palm, and there are millions of these trees on either side of the road for many miles. It seemed inevitable we would eventually come to some processing plant for the production of palm oil, and we did. The oil rendering plant consisted of a group of large black buildings, big furnaces and immense storage tanks. Carts loaded with hearts of the oil palm and pulled by tractors were lined up on the side of the road, waiting to discharge their cargoes for processing.

As we finally approached Quepos we noted a sign pointing the way to the airport. I remarked, "Well, we'll soon be on paved road. They don't build airports serving a major town without building an adequate access road." It was true that the main road was paved, but not before we crossed one more single-lane bridge minus guard rails. The road to the airport was unpaved. How many wrecks are caused by these conditions when *touristas* are trying to make a plane departure at the last *momento?*

We were now on a paved road and after another thirty miles, or so, we came to a crude but very large sign in English directing us to "JACO on the left one kilometer." As we came to what appeared to be the end of the town, we passed a large park lying between the road and the ocean and just beyond the park was the entrance to the Best Western Playa Jaco Club and Resort, all beautifully decorated with lights, garlands and bows for the Christmas season.

Our two bedroom two bath suite was well equipped including a kitchenette with small refrigerator, microwave, coffee pot, toaster, silver and dishes. We had separate views of both the ocean and the mountains. The beach beyond the swimming pool is black volcanic sand and very wide. The music coming from loud speakers around the pool was loud and seemingly constant as a line dancing contest was in progress when we arrived.

As evening approached we realized that the lights in our room were so dim we could barely see. We set out by car to try to find a hundred watt bulb. Driving in the dark on an unlighted unpaved street filled with unlighted bicycles weaving in, out and around the heavy vehicular traffic on a busy street was another heart pounding experience. We did find a bulb in a hardware store, returned safely to our room and fell happily into bed.

The next morning, I was determined to boil eggs in the microwave. This turned out to be an unforgettable learning experience, to say the least. I reasoned that three eggs in a dish with water almost, but not quite covering the eggs should take about three minutes to become soft boiled. This was a huge mistake. At about two minutes one of the eggs exploded with a very large BANG. I opened the door of the microwave and the interior looked like a miniature battle scene with egg splattered all over the place. We breakfasted on the hard cooked remains.

The maids cleaned up the mess with no complaint, and pointed out that the light over the desk would not work unless we plugged it back in where we had the computer plugged, and then left us with towels worked into two swans kissing in such a way that beaks and bodies formed a heart. I thought it both clever and kind and took a picture to record it. Over our time in Costa Rica we saw a great variety of such towel sculptures.

We decided to go to the local pharmacy for deodorant and dental floss. The pharmacist did not speak or understand much English, but Dottie completed our purchases by (1) waving her hand under her raised arm, smelling it and making a face, and (2) by simulating flossing her teeth.

The following morning, as we passed the front desk on our way out to the car, the clerk called out, "Is that your green car out there? We want you to move it so we can use fireworks on the birds this evening." We didn't understand immediately, but when we got to the car, we saw why. The car was literally covered with bird droppings from the tree above us! Our green car was now colored with a mixture of gray and white guano.

Despite our filthy car, we decided to take an exploratory ride toward the north and saw a sign reading "Marriott". After a couple of false starts on back roads we came to the newly completed hotel and casino and had a nice view of the golf course. We parked a short way from the entrance to the hotel and stepped into the unbelievably spacious lobby. Dottie remarked, "It's a good thing we didn't park under the portmanteau or they would have thrown us out."

We drove to the marina and yacht club where millions of dollars worth of motor yachts were moored, and then ventured around the various parts of the development until we finally arrived at another area of the extensive property where the entrance resembled a Roman ruin. Overall we took a few pictures and headed for home. It was getting dark, but, as we drove back to Jaco we did stop to take a picture of a house profusely decorated and lighted for the Christmas season.

Back at the hotel, we parked the car and started for the hotel entrance. On the way Dottie collared a management type employee who spoke fluent English, and requested that the car be hosed off. He grabbed an attendant who already had a mop in hand and directed him to do the job. Although not perfect, the vehicle looked much better after his treatment.

The next morning after our personally prepared "room service" breakfast we ventured back into town, this time in daylight so we could see where we were going and also get some idea of what the town was like. Dottie felt the need to negotiate the purchase of a hammock in one of about twenty stores stocking them. This process took some hours, at the end of which the merchant refused to take her credit card. She retreated to another vendor who gave her both a better price and agreed to take the credit card. Then it was on to the *farmacia*, since Dottie wanted to test the statement in Fodor's that most of what are prescription drugs in the U.S. can be bought over the counter without a prescription in Costa Rica. In the test, Dottie asked for

Diamox sequels. The pharmacist had to check availability by phone, but came back very soon to say that they could be available the next day. No prescription necessary!

Our open air lunch was a large bowl of cut fruit, and we lingered for some time to watch the passing crowd, a mixture of *touristas* and natives.

We also had finally spotted the real *Super Mercado* of Jaco It was very well-stocked, but since we had all the food we could use in the immediate future we limited our purchases to a couple of bananas for breakfast.

As darkness approached the cacophony of the birds was almost deafening. We parked well away from trees.

Our pleasant days at Jaco finally ended. The drive from Jaco to Tilaran was interesting and uneventful except for the occasional thrill given by motorists and cyclists passing in the face of numerous blind curves and oncoming traffic. The basic pavement color changed from black or white, to a dark red, patched with black and/or white paving.

Perhaps a bit should be said about OSHA. Its representatives would probably die of heart failure before they got anything done in Costa Rica. Scatter rugs are prevalent; potholes large enough to swallow the front end of a car are features of the roads; one-lane bridges have no guard rails and open pits are unfenced.

Our instructions for getting to the Bird House were that the entrance would be immediately after some heavy road construction, and would be well-marked with a sign, "THE BIRD HOUSE". The road construction was obvious, but there was no sign, before, during or after our passing the construction. There was no sign, but after much travel back and forth in the area, we stopped an inquired of a woman busy sweeping an area in front of a gate across a path leading up the mountain if she knew of the Bird House. She informed us that were at the entry to the Bird House and that she was one of the owners.

The establishment was at the top of a steep slope leading up the mountain. There were two parallel eighteen inch wide concrete tracks set with small rocks or pebbles, apparently to give better traction. "Drive up this track to the first level spot you see and park," she said, "Use plenty of power; you'll need it."

Following her instructions, starting gradually, but soon with the throttle at the floorboards, we lunged forward up the threatening slope, struggling to keep the wheels on the narrow tracks through curves and varying slopes, all steep. We managed to stay the course. Finally, there was the promised parking area, a space about 100 feet wide. We pulled onto the level ground and parked in the left of two spaces. We looked at each other, grinned, and heaved sighs of relief. Now we really were there, we thought.

The Bird House

Actually, we had to climb a steep rise from the parking area to the house, an effort that wore us out. The accommodations were adequate and clean, but the cooking facilities and other amenities of a bed-and-breakfast were not there. Of all things, we didn't want to go back down that steep grade to find a restaurant of unknown quality, and then come back to re-climb the mountain in the dark. We ate some crackers and cheese and went to bed.

The next day, a Saturday, we ventured carefully down the mountain and into Nuevo Arenal. The town is quite attractive, partially we are sure, because it is entirely new, replacing the old Arenal, which was flooded when water filled in behind the dam creating Lake Arenal. The houses are fairly uniform, neatly landscaped and in a variety of colors.

Lunch was at "Tom's Pan", a German bakery and restaurant. There are many German immigrants in Costa Rica and they are particularly concentrated in this area. The menu was printed in three languages, Spanish, English and German. We were taken to seats in an open porch-like area and decided on a single order of roast pork, sauerkraut and noodles. There were no other patrons in the restaurant when we arrived, but while we were waiting for our meal, a busload of German tourists arrived, and the place was filled with Teutonic conversation, much laughter and bustling around.

We had wondered how a restaurant of this kind and size could survive in a small town, but it became apparent that there were connections with the tour companies to direct traffic to Tom's Pan; not different from any other tourist area in the world. The Germans were all served a dessert pastry and coffee, all probably by contract with the tour bus company.

I asked whether the restaurant had a newspaper available for its customers. The German proprietor went to the room behind the bakery, fished out of the trash a copy of the *Tico Times* the English language weekly published in San Jose and offered it for c/200. Regular price: c/350. I bought it for something to read and would normally have discarded it as with any other newspaper, but we decided to keep it as one of many souvenirs of our trip.

In looking the town over, we passed the Catholic Church, the city park and then came upon a much smaller church, The Assembly of God. We took a picture of the church and its beautifully carved door, and decided we would attend the service on Sunday although we realized we could not participate fully in the service because of the language barrier.

On Sunday, the worship was entirely in Spanish; long, complicated and divided into three parts, the first of which was almost entirely singing accompanied by musicians playing drums, a saxophone and guitar. This session was interrupted to get the children of the congregation off to an adjoining room for Sunday School. There were thirty-two people present in the gathering, initially including us, the children and the pastor who was the only person present wearing a tie. He was also the only one wearing a white shirt. The second phase of the service was a responsive reading shared by the minister and a parishioner and the third part was the sermon delivered with much enthusiasm by the pastor.

Following the service we were asked with much hand waving to drive an elderly man to "the point, just across the first bridge". Crossing the bridge was only a beginning. Although we had been on rough roads in Costa Rica, this was the roughest up until that time. The two kilometers up the mountain to the old gentleman's home almost shook us apart, but we made it, and then went back to shop in town.

After some adventures in the area on Monday, as we were preparing for bed, I discovered the car keys were missing. It was black outside, and I dared not venture down the slope to the car.

Tuesday morning, without waiting to exercise, I headed for the car, wire clothes hanger in hand, intending, if necessary, to lift the internal lock button but hoping to find the lost keys en route. However, the keys were locked in the car. No window would move enough to allow my wire to enter. While I was fussing at the car Patrick left to deliver one of his high priced dogs to a lady in San Jose. I wrote down the license plate, the car model, type, and all the name plate data I could find and then came back to the house to request that Charlotte call Patrick, wherever he was, to alert him to the situation and prepare him to pick up a key at the airport if he could. In the meantime we would attempt to contact the car rental agency. The only phone in the house was upstairs in the bedroom area and this was very inconvenient. Time was marching on, but I finally persuaded our hostess to try to call Patrick.

"We used to have one somewhere," was the response when I asked for a phone book so I could contact the car rental office, and the search was on, but a phone book was never found. I did have a card from Sol Tropicale, so I dialed Mark Ayala there. Many rings on each of the two numbers on the card went unanswered; after all, it was the day before Christmas, but finally a sleepy Mark answered, and following a bit of conversation he agreed to call us back with the needed phone number, "after he had a shower."

He did better than that. After a few minutes, he called, and gave us the necessary number. He also reported that he had called EuroCar, and identified us, himself, the car and Patrick Gabriel to one Jose. Jose promised to provide the necessary keys to Patrick upon his providing proper identification. GREAT RELIEF!!

Charlotte called a cab, and invited Dottie to ride downtown with her. I was surprised there was cab service in such a small town, but even more surprised when the cabbie negotiated the climb right up to Patrick's parking spot next to the house. This broke up the day somewhat. Finally, at 4:30 Patrick appeared and the keys worked.

At this point Charlotte announced that we all were invited to a neighbor's home for a Christmas Eve party. "The neighbors' house is just down the road", meaning down the mountain to the main road, and then on downward toward the lake. An entry drive a few yards down the road from the Bird House gate would lead us to the party. It was then four forty-five and she said we were to be there at five o'clock. Why we weren't informed earlier was never made clear. Patrick announced he was tired and not going. Charlotte announced she had planned to take a turkey to the party, "But hadn't had time to fix it." Instead she quickly mixed a bunch of juices in a gallon cooler and we started out.

What ensued was one of the craziest evenings in our lives. "You drive," directed Charlotte to me. We descended the mountain in second gear once again, crossed the main road and proceeded down a concrete drive just broader than the span of our wheels. This narrow road wound down the mountain in sharp curves and abrupt descents until at the bottom we were in what looked like a conventional subdivision overlooking Lake Arenal. There was no party; only a cigar smoking resident holding a glass of whiskey in his hand. A woman in a bathing suit arrived from the nearby pool and informed us (1) Her name was Terry (2) she was badly hung over from the previous night's party, and (3) tonight's party would start later. With that she invited us to explore her house, which she shared with the cigar-smoking whiskey drinker.

When the party eventually began, it was attended by a group of people of astonishingly disparate nationalities. The host, Klaus, was German, as was his mother, visiting from Germany, a lady who was almost exactly our age. Klaus is married to Betty, a beautiful Costa Rican woman, some years younger than Klaus. She had originally owned the land on which the subdivision stood. We learned that Klaus had previously subdivided smaller pieces of property in the area, and when he ran out of property to develop he began to eye the large vacant area that had been inherited by Betty. It appeared that a marital/financial arrangement followed.

A second Terry, male, about fifty, was married to a Costa Rican girl about seventeen or eighteen. This Terry had his hair tied up in a top knot like the Indian guide in *"The Last of the Mohicans"*. Brian Tuttle was a Brit, living in Spain, who was visiting for a week. Charlotte spent most of the evening talking to a lady from Finland, who spends winters at her condo on Lake Arenal. John, from Seattle, and his Panamanian wife were also present.

After we all had had a couple of drinks, either beer or wine, the male Terry started cooking some marinated beef on a gas barbecue. The female Terry reappeared after having had a swim, fully dressed in a long red dress. The group was seated at two tables. Dottie and I were served a dinner of the barbecued beef, potato and a small bit of highly spiced guacamole. It became painfully apparent that Charlotte's turkey was sorely missed. We shared our bit of beef with the fellow from Spain and Klaus's mother, both of whom were seated at our table. The others ate potatoes, guacamole and dark bread, and drank some of Charlotte's smoothie, which had to substitute for the anticipated turkey.

The conversation was animated, and covered a great variety of subjects, but nothing on world politics. For the most part, Klaus presided. John sat holding his head. This was a different kind of Christmas Eve, to say the least.

The darkness closed in about us, although the patio was well lighted. About seven thirty three well-dressed young women appeared, one of whom was Betty's daughter. The girls were on their way to a Christmas Eve party. There were greetings, introductions all around and much laughter.

Shortly thereafter the affair ended abruptly, and all left. The lights went out on the patio and pool areas, and we were standing in utter blackness next to the car. I screwed my courage up to the sticking point, and we started up the tortuous trail to the main road, and thence onward and upward to the Bird House. We made it, and heaved a sigh of relief, but we had yet to struggle up the difficult trail to our quarters. In the process, Dottie kicked the axle of the native cart which decorated the slope and suffered a painful laceration.

Our days were spent exploring the interesting areas around Lake Arenal, including cattle ranches, fruit groves, and interesting little stores and restaurants.

The Gabriels announced that they were going to take us to dinner at the hot springs below Arenal volcano on New Year's Eve, and then they took great pains to inform us that each couple would pay its own expenses. They announced we would be leaving about four o'clock but we really didn't get underway until about four forty-five. I drove, with the promise that Patrick would be allowed to drive home. The drive to the restaurant included a road over the top of the dam which creates Lake Arenal. The dam itself is quite an engineering feat, and it is further unique in that the entire project reverses the flow of a river from the Atlantic to the Pacific.

All cars at the springs are backed into their spaces, allowing for a quick getaway in case the volcano erupts. As there were hundreds, if not thousands, of people in and around the resort, with all of its ancillary activities, one can only imagine what chaos would result if the volcano gave forth with a major eruption. Actually, it is in a state of minor eruption virtually all of the time.

The restaurant, which overlooks a part of the steaming hot springs, was jammed with people. There was some kind of a foul-up with regard to our reservation, but Patrick slipped the maitre d' a few *colones*, and we were seated immediately. Dottie and I each had a cocktail, and "Doc" and "Charlie" each had a fruit drink from the buffet. The Gabriels seemed to be very anxious to get on with the meal. That was probably just as well, for at about that time two or more busses unloaded their passengers, and all occupants headed for the buffet. Although jostling prevailed, we managed to get what we wanted – dark meat from the turkey, a piece of steak, bread and some vegetables. We managed to get back to the table struggling through the crowd.

Charlie once again disappeared into the mass of humanity pressing along the buffet tables. Doc was at our table momentarily, but headed off for the dessert table. He made two trips, bringing back, in total, four pieces of chocolate cake, three pieces of pumpkin pie, and two sundae glasses of a nut-filled custard. Finally, Charlotte reappeared carrying two heavily overloaded plates of food for herself.

By then Dottie and I had almost finished our dinners, and it didn't take our friends long to polish off theirs. We each had a small piece of cake and they ate every bite of the rest of the desserts. Doc wrapped up a couple of turkey leg bones for their house dogs. We paid our check by Visa; Doc laid out a one hundred dollar bill and got back a pile of colones, both paper and coin.

Then it was off to inspect the volcano hot springs. It was like the movie versions of the hereafter, with swirling steam everywhere. People were sitting under the falling waters, immersed in the pools, and some were jumping in and out of the water Another part of the property features an immense swimming pool, heated to one hundred four degrees Fahrenheit by the volcano. The whole was immersed in clouds of steam through which one could vaguely see people and their surroundings. It struck me as being like the movie versions of the hereafter.

By agreement, despite our concerns about the insurance on the car which specified that only I would drive, Doc drove home, never once driving over forty-three kilometers per hour and all the while, i.e. about an hour and a half, delivering a monologue on the state of world affairs.

The skies were almost cloudless, a rare condition around the volcanoes themselves. We stopped to photograph this scene.

The next day, with our stay at the Bird House behind us, we set out for the Caribbean side of the country. On our way, we stopped as we approached the dam to get a couple of pictures of the volcano, which was almost cloudless, an unusual phenomenon. Dozens of cars were stopped there, and many people were wandering around. We soon shoved onward. Very soon, the terrain evened off and the driving was greatly improved.

A sign clearly indicated the direction to Guapiles. The name of this town is pronounced "wah-pah-leez", but we persisted in calling it "gooey-piles" in our private conversations in the car. We stopped and enjoyed a beautiful steak for lunch after which we were on the well-paved main road once again. It was after five o'clock when we rolled off the highway and onto the dirt streets of Cahuita. As we were now well east of San Jose, and even more easterly of Arenal, the sun was already setting. A quick inquiry sent us to the police station and from there to El Encanto, where the host, who was looking for us, opened the gate.

The proprietor, Pierre, and his wife, Patricia, carried our luggage, and we followed them along a decorative, winding concrete path through lawn surrounded by tropical foliage to our well-appointed cabin. The woodwork, furniture and ceilings were entirely of knotless mahogany. The wall decorations were tasteful, including a large mosaic with a Buddhist theme. After being offered a soft drink or beer, we asked for some bread and were given six slices of delicious whole grain homemade bread, some cheese, butter and marmalade, and this comprised our supper. We fell exhausted into bed and slept for ten hours.

Our hostess, Patricia, was a Chinese Canadian; Pierre a French Canadian. Both are Buddhists and the environment displayed that culture, both indoors and out. The living and dining areas are under roof, but open to the surrounding gardens. The tables are all of teak. The room beyond the dining area contains numerous Chinese artifacts, comfortable lounges and a considerable library, all for guests of El Encanto to enjoy.

We spent five pleasant days exploring around Cahuita, including a visit to a Dole processing plant, the Dole harbor, where large refrigerator ships are docked while loading pineapples, and a trip around the mountain lying just north of the river marking the border between Costa Rica and Panama. One of our explorations was a guided tour in the company of a Swiss couple, but we found some of the activities a bit much for us.

One of these was a visit to a village of the native Indian people across a river at the bottom of a deep ravine. Access to the village required crossing a deep ravine on a rope bridge. As we approached the ravine, we looked up, and sure enough, there was a cable-supported bridge across that ravine. In order to get on it, one had to climb about thirty swaying steps, supported by the cables leading to the bridge. The bridge itself had rough-hewn planks, laid in pairs, across the entire span. This looked like a challenge to all of us, but the Swiss couple quickly conquered their fears and climbed up to cross the river. With every step they took on the bridge, it swung under them in an arc which extended perhaps three feet on either side. I crossed shakily over, but Dottie declined.

Thursday, January second we planned to eat at seven thirty and be on our way by nine, but due to the fact our hosts had been New Year celebrants along with the rest of the town, our breakfast was not ready until after eight. Perhaps as a gesture of apology for the lateness of the meal, or penance for their behavior, we were served plates of sunny side eggs, whole wheat toast as well as the beautiful fruit.

So, as those things go, it was ten o'clock before we had put all of our things in order, and David, our hosts' son, put them in the car. Although we had said our adieus to Pierre and Patricia earlier, after we had opened the gate and climbed into the car, Pierre suddenly appeared at the car window, gave the Buddhist symbol of peaceful greeting, wished us a safe journey, and handed us a pound of a special Costa Rican coffee as a farewell. We were off to cross the continental divide once again.

We climbed up to the continental divide on highway thirty-two. This was the best road we had been on in Costa Rica. It was three-laned for all up grades, the lanes were wider than almost all other roads, and best of all, no potholes! Steep grades and sharp turns remained with us, however, as we climbed through the most intense rain forest, with its immense leaves and giant ferns until we were above the level where oxygen would be necessary if we stayed for any extended time. Only occasionally could we see beyond the encircling forest to the mountains around us or to the valleys below. Suddenly, the rain forest was behind us, and we made our way back to the Best Western Iruzu. The next day after another three hour flight, we exited the aircraft in West Palm Beach, and our driver was there waving a placard with "BERTSCH" displayed upon it. In an hour and a half we were home and Costa Rica was a pleasant memory.

FRANCE (19)
Departure in a Hurricane

Dottie's cousin Elaine, although of German extraction, was enamored of France the French, their language and their culture. She had studied in France for several years early in life and earned a master's degree at the Sorbonne, an achievement of which she was intensely proud. Following her Pittsburgh marriage to Leslie Armstrong, a brilliant metallurgical engineer, the couple moved to the Chicago area where Les worked his magic in developing a variety of special aluminum alloys for customers of Alcoa, at that time the Aluminum Corporation of America.

Exercising her French language skill, Elaine taught French at a university in the Chicago area for a number of years. When this talented couple had reached a financial position that would enable them to enjoy a few luxuries, they moved to Crete, Illinois bought a house, joined the local country club where Elaine, not previously a golfer, took lessons in order to play with Les, who was already an accomplished golfer.

The couple prospered financially and eventually began talking about the possibility of owning a vacation home somewhere. To Elaine this meant a country place in France. To Les it meant a place in a golfing community. The accommodation of these two positions meant a country place in Southern France on a golf course open for play all year long. While all this occurred long before I knew them, as far as I know, no one factored in the long-term cost of flaying back and forth for their vacations.

On the several occasions when Dottie and I were with them, both before and after our marriage, one or both of them would say, "You must come and visit us when we're in France." After our Hawaii and Costa Rica adventures, a trip to France and a leisurely time on a golf course in Southern France sounded ideal. We a;so planned to join our hosts if possible for a day or so in Paris before proceeding to our their vacation home in a development on the Mediterranean close to the border with Spain. The tentative Paris rendezvous was made uncertain by the fact that we would be flying "Space Available" in a military plane, a privilege I had as a result of my naval service. While this made overseas travel inexpensive, the cost per flight being about a dollar and a half for a military box lunch, there were many uncertainties, such as having space on a flight to or near one's desired destination, or having no space at all.

It was necessary for the space "A" passengers to be present a couple of hours before flight time, where names are called in accordance with established priorities, of which space "A" is the lowest. When we judged it was about time for us to get to Dover Air Force Base and establish our names on the priority list, we left the shack, drove to the base, parked our car in long-term parking and proceeded to the Military Air Transport Service Terminal, where we saw to it we were on the general list for departures, with preferences for flights to Paris, Spain or England. If we couldn't get to Paris, Spain was a good alternative, as Ste. Cyprien is just across the Spanish border in France, and the Spanish railway system would get us to the border from anywhere we landed in Spain.

We had been aware of the usual reports iof hurricanes in the Caribbean and the Atlantic, but thought it unlikely our plans would be affected. We seated ourselves in the Space A waiting room, watched television, chatted with the other prospective travelers and ventured occasionally to the desk to check on our place on the last. After a couple of hours it looked as though we would be able to get on a scheduled flight to Paris, as we were close to the top of the list. Not long after that there was an announcement that the flight to Paris was cancelled, followed shortly with an announcement that the Bachelor Officers Quarters was full, and could accept no more residents, due to flight cancellations, "Occurring because of the approaching hurricane."

This announcement was the first official mention of the hurricane threat, but it was followed by others advising MATS passengers to seek shelter. We felt secure because we had reserved a room at the BOQ, but even that might be threatened if enough active duty personnel needed a place to sleep. The terminal was rapidly emptying when I went to the desk to determine what our situation might be. "All flights have been cancelled except for a high priority flight to Ramstein, Germany. If it goes, there will be space for fifteen Space A passengers. We added our names to the list and sat down, somewhat apprehensively to see if the flight was a "go."

By this time it was dark and rain was driving down in sheets. I doubted we would get out of Dover, but finally the call came to proceed to a room where our passports and baggage were checked, and shortly thereafter we boarded a bus for transportation to the plane, a huge C5. The plane, with its starboard engines already running at low speed, seemed mountainous in the glare of the lights shining on the plane on the tarmac. Two flights of temporary stairs led up what on a land locked building would be about four stories to an open hatch. Climbing those stairs was a bit of a struggle for people of our age, but we made it, and were seated over the cargo area facing the rear of the plane.

When we were in the air, the Air National Guardsmen who formed the crew of the aircraft, including it pilots, made every effort to make us comfortable, issued us pillows and blankets, and announced that the box lunches we had paid for would be distributed after about the first third of the flight. After eating we slept for the final two thirds of the flight until just before landing. We were in Germany, but we were there many days before our scheduled rendezvous with the Armstrongs.

It was well into the afternoon, but we managed to get a rental car, thinking we might drive to Paris. That plan turned out to be impractical. We registered for a stay in the bachelor officers quarters and were assigned a luxury room reserved for officers at or above my rank.. We then used some of those days to drive around that area of Germany and were impressed by the beauty of the countryside and how well kept the private homes were. We bought what we thought would be enough U.S. Military dollar denoted certificates to get along for a few days and also pay for our train tickets to Paris.

One of the evenings at Ramstein we were invited to a promotion party for air force officers who had been selected for the rank of lieutenant colonel. It was a gala event and much appreciated. Another evening we enjoyed a meal at a famous nearby restaurant that served all of Germany's fines breads, sausages and other foods for a flat rate.

Finally it was time to catch the Paris express at nearby railroad station. We allowed plenty of time to turn in the rental car and get to the station before the scheduled arrival of the train. We took our seats in the waiting room with a number of other passengers and I then got into the line outside the ticket window. Time was going by and I kept checking my watch to judge the rate at which the line advanced. Finally I was looking through the grilled window and plunked down enough of the military certificates to pay for the tickets to Paris.

The clerk behind the counter pushed the certificates back at me and said. "*Nein*," and then a flow of other German I could not understand. A friendly bilingual German behind me said, "What the clerk is saying is that the national railroad will only accept German marks and he cannot accept your military money. You will have to go to the bank down the street and exchange your certificates for marks. I think the bank down the street is open for about another fifteen minutes."

He gave me directions to the bank and I set off in a trot, hoping I would not be standing in another line when I got there. There was no line, so I went up to the first window and pushed my certificates across the marble counter to the clerk, who promptly returned to me the proper amount of marks, less an exchange fee. I ran back to the train station and found myself behind another line with only a few minutes before the arrival of the train. I would never make it up to the counter on time. I looked around for my German friend, but he was nowhere to be seen.

About then the ticket clerk stepped out of his cage and shouted, "Paris, Paris," and waved toward his work station. I raced to accept his invitation and was clutching the proper tickets as the train sped into the station.

The ride to the frontier was like flying and amazingly smooth. We enjoyed a lunch and shortly were at the border, where the German crew was exchanged for French personnel and we continued our trip to Paris, where we grabbed a cab for the hotel, which we understood was just a short distance from the station. We had a few hundred francs, but were reluctant to spend them, as Les had told us that the exchange rate in Ste. Cyprian was much more favorable than in Paris.

The taxi driver put his hand out and demanded payment of far more than the fare should have been, so I simply escorted Dottie into the hotel followed by the driver. The owner of this small hotel, serving also as the concierge, was expecting us and soon settled the fare for about a third of what the driver had demanded. We were greatly impressed by the little elevator that would barely accommodate us with our limited baggage.

Les and Elaine soon joined us and we spent three or four days exploring Paris and enjoying al fresco lunches. We were amazed at the prices of everything, a considerable shock to this thrifty Dutchman, but I kept a stiff upper lip and let the francs and dollars flow onto our Visa card.

Les and Elaine left a half day before we were to board the sleeper train for Saint Cyprian at Paris Sud. We had purchased tickets for this leg of the journey a few days earlier and expected to board the train as soon as the sleepers were available, but no, it was then required to purchase sleeping accommodations; our tickets were for transportation only. When we did finally board the train, we found we were sharing a compartment with a genial Frenchman, who offered us a drink of wine. Later, after we were well on our way southward we offered him a drink of bourbon from our limited supply, but when he put the glass to his lips and took a tastes, he said, "No, no, no bourbon *por moi*" and handed the glass back to me for disposal.

There was a large crowd pf people at the station when the train rolled into Ste. Cyprian and it appeared to us that the gathering was either some kind of minor festival or a farmers' market, as there were tables set up with things to sell things ranging from vegetables to household goods. Les was nowhere to be seen, and an hour passed. In our experience Les was always on time or even a bit early for any appointment, and this gave us additional concern. It was not like him. We tried phoning the Ste. Cyprian number they had given us, but had no success. We finally took seats in the station waiting room, and after a time I decided to cross the street to the local hotel to inquire about the availability of rooms and was assured that shelter would be available if we need it.

Another hour or two passed and we became resigned to our fate; Les would show up sometime, perhaps tomorrow.

And then he suddenly appeared at a three fourths hour mark and expressed considerable surprise that we were already there; By his calculation the train would be arriving in another twenty minutes. We never did figure out how it could be that Les, a man of precision could be so late, but a part of the time could be accounted for by the fact that Les always carried Greenwich mean time on his watch.

It was a pleasant drive of an hour or so to the Armstrong's country club dwelling which we expected to be an impressive establishment not dissimilar to their home in Crete. Our expectation was about as wrong as possible. Our cousins' golf course home was of a design that only a golf addict could love, and while adequate for a couple, was totally inadequate for more. We entered directly into a rather small room that turned out to be the living room. As we passed a space to our left that I thought to be a closet, Les said, "You may put your things in here," and deposited the suitcase he was carrying for us.

A quick tour of the premises included a peek into the Pullman kitchen from which a door opened directly on the golf course. A set of almost vertical steps led upward from the living room to the only bathroom in the place, and Les explained that their bedroom was also up there. There was not room for all of us to explore that upper region at the same time, so Dottie ventured the climb and returned wondering how one could possibly execute that climb in the middle of the night. I had already concluded that for my part, the golf course was going to get a little extra watering. It was only at the end of this tour that I realized the closet where we had deposited our bags was our assigned sleeping space. There was no other.

There were two narrow bunks in that closet, with rope mesh supporting mattresses filled with straw. Dottie took the upper bunk and promptly went to sleep, but when I got into the lower bunk the ropes went to the floor and the straw mattress provided little cushioning from the ropes that cut into my back. Somehow I survived the night and the next day sought out whatever pillows were available, including those on the sofa.

My lower back had continued to deteriorate over the several years since the operation to alleviate some of the stress on my upper back, and I really could not walk the golf course without considerable pain, so I read and visited with some of the neighbors, all interesting people, mostly English.

Under my influence Les had become an avid Rotarian and made up his attendance regularly at the Wednesday meeting of the Rotary Club of Ste. Cyprian, the railroad terminus where we had waited so long before being escorted to the Armstrong cottage. On our arrival at the club venue, about fifteen minutes before the scheduled meeting time, Les was greeted like a long lost brother, and we were forthwith served glasses of red wine.

Les wandered among the club members, speaking to many of them in what could only be described Franglish or perhaps Fractured French, part English, part French, and it was obvious he had developed great rapport with this group during his vacation times in France. When I was addressed with,

"*Parlez vous Francaise?*" I would reply, based on my four years of college French, "*Un peu.*"

The result of those encounters was, quite naturally, an invitation to address a few words in French to the club when introduced. I had a bit of time to prepares, and so was able to address the club in a few sentences of less that perfect French starting with, "*Bonjour mes amis Rotarins. Je suis le frere de Rotarian Armstrong...*" and a few more sentences. My pronouncement was greeted with lengthy applause. Although every member of the club spoke English as well as French, it was obviously important to them that I at least make an attempt to speak to them in their language.

Our final adventure on French soil was a short drive through rugged mountain terrain to the Spanish border, where we were greeted by a friendly Spanish border guard, but decided not to enter Spain and view a continuations of the rocky scene.

Upon return to Ste. Cyprian we called MATS and were told that because of heavy traffic to and from the rest of Europe, our best bet for travel back to the States would be to get to Rota, at that time a U. S. Naval Air Station in southwestern Spain, and after a few, at least to us, hair raising experiences with the Spanish rail system, we arrived at the naval station, where were told the next flight to the U. S. would not depart until four days after our arrival, if then, and that the possibility of our getting on board was minimal. We got a room in the BOQ and checked with flight operations morning, noon and night for two days always receiving negative responses, but on the morning of the third day the airman on the other end of the line said, "There is a flight coming in from Italy en route to the States. We don't know if there'll be any Space A seats. But you'd best be down here by noon to find out."

At eleven thirty we were at the terminal. The plane was equipped as a troop carrier. There would be room for us and several other passengers, we were told, but there were no facilities on board for civilian passengers other than a short barrel equipped with a toilet seat, the privacy of which was provided by a tarpaulin slung from hooks on the skin of the plane. A crewman announced, "There are no bucket seats. If you go, you will be seated on the troop seating with which this plane is equipped, canvas stretched across aluminum tubing along either side of the interior of the plane. The remainder of the space behind the cockpit will be filled with cargo. Box lunches are available for a buck and a half apiece." Although Dottie was somewhat apprehensive, we took the flight; there really were no viable alternatives.

Our destination was Naval Air Station Lakehurst, New Jersey not Dover, so a train ride was necessary to get us back to our car. On arrival at Dover, we discovered that our car had a flat tire and it was another minor adventure to get it changed and repaired, but eventually we were back at the shack reminiscing about the great time we had in France and Germany.

HOMECOMING (20)
"They Haven't Lost a Foundation Yet."

The annual Wells Tannery Homecoming was a July event that had been a highlight of the year for several generations. The valley residents had always done all of the work in connection with the celebration, but this year there was some doubt about whether there would be enough participation to make the affair a success. The inhabitants of the valley who had volunteered for years to fill the many jobs in connection with the homecoming were getting older and a bit reluctant to put forth the effort to produce the event once again. There were few younger people to fill in, since there were no jobs in the valley other than farming, and thus most young people departed the valley upon high school graduation seeking a way to make a living. They were inclined to return for the event, but felt no strong inclination to work at it.

There were other problems. Residents of the valley were expected to make cash contributions to sponsor the event, and it was hard to get someone to do the necessary soliciting. The mess hall would have to be cleaned a few days before the event, and the area to be used for parking would have to be mowed. Individuals and organizations to participate in the parade would have to be contacted and encouraged to participate, and now time was passing by as the usual date for the homecoming approached. Several of the long-time supporters of the event called a meeting and exhorted the attendees to take action, and somehow within the next few weeks, all of the preparations were made and people from all over poured into the village for a festive day..

Fire engines that would be the pride of most metropolitan fire departments headed the Wells Valley Homecoming Parade as the procession wended its way down Wells Tannery Road for the parade's first pass through the village. In this first event of the annual Wells Valley Homecoming, many additional highly sophisticated pieces of fire equipment were interspersed with the other units of the parade coming down the main stem of Wells Tannery; Breezewood Pumper #6, Six Mile Run Ladder #9, Houstontown Chemical #8, and so forth. In addition, there were all-purpose fire trucks and mobile units especially equipped to fight brush and forest fires. All wee a highly-polished bright red, glistening in the sun, and each carried a few volunteer firemen tossing assorted wrapped candies, bubble gum and a variety of other goodies, mostly intended for the children, among the spectators lining the mile-long main stretch of road on which most of the village houses front. "They've never seen a fire they didn't like, and they've never lost a foundation yet," remarked one jokester observing the scene.

Dottie and I went almost an hour early for this eleven o'clock event, but found the road into the village already blocked with a temporary barricade guarded by a sheriff's deputy, who let us pass when we convinced him with a wave that we were going to the celebration. "Enjoy the homecoming," he shouted with a smile. After descending the quarter mile grade into the village, we parked our car well off to one side on the vacant lot next to the Horton house, pulled our folding chairs out of the trunk and set them next to the road in the shade of the big maple tree in the Horton yard across from the church.

People on the porches of the houses on both sides the road, are shouted greetings to folks walking past in both directions. Across the road from us, next to the church, the driveway of a house slopes upward at a considerable angle such that it is quite a climb from the street up the porch, while the back of the house is at ground level. From the porch a man shouted, "Hey, Dorothy! Do you remember me? I'm John Chamberlain, an' we used to play together when we was kids and you come up here from Pittsburgh fer the summer. Later on I worked fer your Dad when he was rebuilding that house of his where you now live. It's a real homecoming and reunion for me." Dottie dutifully walked across the street to greet her childhood friend, while I sat down to rest my weary back.

On her return, Dottie was greeted by a woman so tall I thought she should be playing professional basketball. "Hi, Dot, see you next Friday." She is Dottie's local hairdresser, Rita Wright, who is independent enough that she only schedules customers two days a week. They talked about children and grandchildren. Dottie told her about her great grandchildren. Everyone is interested in the well being of everyone in the community. As she left Rita repeated, "See ya Friday."

Dottie said, "I'm going down to the post office to mail these letters and see if there's any mail." The post office is at the corner of Wells Tannery Road and Cove Road, one hundred percent downtown, if there is one. This intersection is perhaps three hundred feet from where we established up our little observation station. I nodded an acknowledgement to Dottie and fumbled with my camera, hoping to get some good pictures of the parade. Numerous kids on bicycles flew down the parade route, shouting at each other and at the crowd.

After a time, Dottie returned with a bundle of mail, mostly junk, and I walkrd it over to the car. "The new postmaster is Laurie Baird from Roaring Springs, and the new assistant is Bonnie Pittman from Hopewell," Dottie reported on her return. "We had quite a chat about how things are going down there with both of them new to the job."

Ray Koontz, who shares a pew with us in church, stopped by to pass the time of day.

Meanwhile, the Moseby clan pulled up in a huge SUV, and Edith, the ninety-three year old matron of the family, was assisted to a chair by son Bill and grandson Jeff, while the rest of the group, Bill's wife, Carolyn, granddaughter, Tracey, and her husband, Dave Nuner; daughter Florence and her husband, Bob Pyle, took their places at the side of the road.

Edith greeted us with the comment, "It's wonderful that it cooled off a bit; I don't think I would have made it if it was going to be a hundred again today," and we then discussed the weather, the status of the corn crop, the problem of the increasing deer population, the crowd at the Center Church Ice

Cream Social the week before last, and how good the food and ice cream were there.

Sitting on the ground between me and their parents were three little girls, ages about three to ten, anxiously waiting for the parade to start. I tried to engage them in conversation with the standard, "How old are you?"

They answered with one word apiece in inverse order of age, "Nine", "Six", "Three."

I tried again, "Where do you live?" and got a two word answer in unison, "Three Springs." We could hear a band playing in the distance, signaling that the parade was about to begin. The little girls became far more friendly as I helped them to retrieve the handfuls of candy that started to rain down in front of us hurled by the friendly firemen in the shining fire trucks leading the parade into the village.

In the units following were beautiful horses and ponies ridden by men, women and children gussied up in their Western clothing. The beautiful animals pranced gracefully along the route. Several of the men are carryied children too young to ride themselves. Next came a group of scantily clad youngsters, primarily girls, intermittently twirling batons to the sound of recorded band music blaring from the roof of an accompanying pickup truck. The group ranged in age from tiny tots to eighteen-year-old beauties. The little ones were worn out by the time the twirlers complete their first excursion through the village and are then carried for the rest of the distance by accompanying adults, These budding drum majorettes marched behind a hand-lettered banner carried by a couple of members of the group proclaiming them to be "The Breezewood Twirlers."

John Ford, riding in a wheel barrow pushed by his son-in-law, and dressed in what are intended to look like baby clothes, followed the twirlers. The township supervisor was licking a very large "all day sucker" and was towing behind the wheelbarrow one of his coon dogs on a leash. His constituents loved it, clapped their hands and whistled. Behind the Post Office, the rest of John's coon hounds, several dozen in number, stood outside their cobbled-up dog houses along the creek, heads in the air, and set up a clamor in response to all the sounds from the parade route; the music, the cheering, the clapping, the occasional booing and the inevitable smart remarks from both the audience and participants, together with all the other noises generated by the parade and its audience, broke the usual quietude of the village.

After a few more fire trucks interspersed with new cars, trucks, tractors and other motorized farm implements, all manned by personnel from the represented selling agencies, and prominently displaying advertising, a real band struttrf down the road. It is the Forbes Road High School Band, and it played real marching music.

Following the band, on a farm trailer pulled by one of Tim Moseby's tractors from the Lost Creek Implement Company, driven by nephew Jeff, was a miniature replica of Wells Valley Presbyterian Church large enough to fill most of the trailer, towering over a group of Sunday School children riding on the float. One of the kiddoes, pullied on a rope, yo keep the bell in the church belfry ringing to attract attention to the sign reading, "Join us for services and Sunday School on Sunday morning." This float, with various remodelings and improvements, carrying the church's invitation to attend services, has been in the annual parade for years, with no noticeable effect on the Sunday attendance, which ranges from twenty to thirty worshippers weekly.

After another section of advertising vehicles caome the float of the Wells Valley Methodist Church, located a couple of miles outside the village down State Road 913. Their float featured a small organ and a group of people dressed in period clothing, the men in black suits and ties wearing stove pipe hats, and the women in long printed dresses, their heads covered with bonnets or tatted "covers". An invitation to attend the Methodist Church services, lettered on a placard reads, " Join us on Sunday. We have a church service & Sunday School every Sunday, and a real preacher every third Sunday," an indication that the congregation shares an ordained minister with two other churches. Attendance doesn't seem to be much better there than in the village church. Someone once suggested that the two churches in the valley combine their efforts, and was rebuffed by both camps. The concept of "Unity in Christ" does not seem to have any effect, here or elsewhere. A third church, halfway in between the two, roof sagging and paint peeling, has been without services for years, another symbol of decaying attendance.

The parade wended its way through the loop of road on which the village lies, and then made a second pass through the lines of spectators to its point of origin. A few units dropped out on the second pass and made their way down to the picnic grounds, where the smoke from the barbecue pits was wafting delicious odors toward the crowd, inviting everyone to participate in the eating orgy that would soon be underway there.

At the park, in preparation for the big event, and to provide parking for the hundreds of cars, trucks, SUV's and campers flocking to Wells Tannery, the outfield of the baseball diamond has been mowed all the way out to the entrance, where a large hand lettered sign read "Wells Valley Park –Everyone Welcome – No Alcoholic Beverages Permitted – Enter at Your Own Risk." Some folks will stay for the day, and some will stay just for the lunch. Others arrived for the events later in the day. Constant movement of vehicles and people, with children running and chasing each other incessantly, was prevalent. Groups stood and chatted, renewing old acquaintanceships, some folks not having seen each other for a year or more. Other groups sat on the benches scattered around the grounds doing the same.

Wells Creek, which originates from a spring behind the village, runs along the western boundary of the park at the edge of the state forest that occupies most of the thousands of acres of woods lying between Wells Tannery and Breezewood. A few kids attending the homecoming waded in the creek, while groups of youngsters pushed and shoved each other trying to force someone into the water. Along the creek, there are two permanent open air roofed shelters, one used as a band stand, and the other for various uses, but often, during homecoming, occupied by one or the other of the visiting fire companies to sell, for the benefit of their organization, various food item such as ice cream, candy and snack items not directly in competition with the food being served in the dining hall.

The dining hall, a concrete block structure large enough to hold several hundred people seated at tables includes, in addition to the dining area, a substantial kitchen and serving facility, where food preparation has been underway since early morning. Between the hall and the creek is the barbecue pit, where a hundred split spring chicken halves have been roasting over charcoal for a couple of hours, with several hundred more yet to be started through the process stacked nearby. Savory aromas have drifted across the whole scene and are luring the hungry homecoming folks. Twenty-five chicken halves at a time are pressed between large framed wire grates having two handles on each side so the barbecue cooks can turn the whole frame frequently during the grilling process. Four such frames of chicken are atop the pits at any given time.

Presiding over this operation was the same Pete Ford who is the church elder and greeter, Republican State Committee Member and generally recognized "good guy". Pete, dripping with sweat, wiped his forehead as we approached, greeted us with a hearty, "Where ya bin? We bin expectin' ya." In response to our inquiry as to whether there will be enough chicken for us to have a serving apiece later in the day, Pete said, "Well, we think there's enough, but when it's gone, it's gone." We thought maybe we should have chicken for both the noon and supper meals. As we leave, Pete sprayed the roasting chicken halves with a basting mixture from a Spray'n'Wash bottle and the charcoal flared up briefly.

By this time the first of the two country western groups scheduled for the homecoming was starting to warm up, so we edged up to a picnic table in the shade near the band stand. The "Fulton County Five" included musicians (in a manner of speaking) playing two guitars, a banjo, a keyboard and a fiddle, with the banjo player occasionally alternating on a mandolin. All, including the woman playing the keyboard, wee dressed in western regalia, blue jeans, cowboy hats and prominent red bandanas. As we sat down, most of the band members were tuning their instruments. The banjo player was plucking out a solo version of "I'll Fly Away." The loudspeaker system suddenly let out a howl that could be heard all over the park. Dottie covered her ears, and threatened to move farther away, but the screeching sound was soon subdued.

After a few more squawks and a great deal of tuning, one of the guys stepped forward and said, "We're gonna open up with our theme song, 'Folsom Prison.' Now no smart remarks from the audience, please," and the picking, plucking and singing began.

"Jambalaya," "Your Cheatin' Heart," "No Tear Drops Tonight" and "In the Shadow of the Pines" followed, with intermittent retuning of instruments and a few comments by both audience and instrumentalists. We clapped after each song in appreciation of the musicians' efforts, but very few others did. Many of the listeners were munching on chicken, barbecue sandwiches or other goodies. "My Pauline, a Truck Driver's Queen," drew a bit of applause from a table where someone named Pauline was seated.

Dick Johnson, one of Ron Black's numerous cousins, dropped by for a few minutes. "How ya doin'? Nice day." As always, on the occasion of the homecoming, he was wearing high-heeled western boots, black pants, a leather vest and a cowboy hat. Most of the time he has a toothpick in his mouth and has his thumbs tucked into his three-inch belt with an immense silver buckle and silver baubles imbedded along its entire girth. After a bit more conversation, Dick continued his rounds. He is a sort of circuit rider of the homecoming, and probably would consider he had failed in his duties if he had not spoken at some time during the day to everyone in attendance.

The Fulton County Five continued to belt out its country tunes, "Swimmin' in the Creek," "Seven Spanish Angels," "The

Wreck of the Old Ninety-Seven." A couple sat down across the picnic table from us. The man was wearing a huge black ten gallon hat with a red band, a black shirt and blue jeans. The womam was clad in faded blue bib overalls and a matching blue baseball cap with her long hair protruding from the back of the cap and hanging down to her waist. A boy of about ten, carrying a small guitar and wearing bib overalls sidled up to the end of the table and started strumming the guitar discordantly, but in time with the band playing, " When It's Lamp Lighting Time in the Valley."

We struck up a conversation with the couple, introduced ourselves and found they are Jim & Tess* Aller, members of the "Black Diamond Pickers", a group from the Six Mile Run area up over the mountain past Hopewell, waiting for the time for them to relieve the group currently on the stage. Jim revealed in our conversation that the Pickers play every Friday night at a place called the Black Diamond in Six Mile Run. We had never even heard of the Black Diamond, but think we might like to sample its atmosphere one of these days.

Lined up outside the dining hall were about twenty-five people waiting to get in for the noon meal. The number in line stayed about the same, as people replaced those who were leaving after eating. We had long since decided to wait until there is no line; our backs can't stand the pressure of standing very long. The occupants of the band stand wee playing "How's the World Treatin' You?" as an older man pulled up a folding chair next to us and sat down. Jim introduced him as "Uncle Jack Foor, who plays the fiddle in our group." Uncle Jack beamed a toothless smile our way and cradled a fiddle on his arm.

Tess said, ""I'm hungry. I'm gonna git somethin' to eat," and disappeared through the smoke of the barbecue pit, around the back of the hall, and was back in five minutes with a basketful of french fries and a funnel cake. She evidently used some prerogative of entertainers to skip the waiting line by going in the back door to order the food. The strains of "Folsom Prison," and the words "I Hear the Train a'Comin'…", are filling the air, belted out in a husky voice by the bib overall clad woman strumming her guitar.

The basket of fries melted away rapidly as the Allers dug into it. Uncle Jack, having no teeth, just sucked on a single long fry. "The Trail of the Lonesome Pine" is the next offering from the Fulton Five. A large man wearing striped bib overalls left the small audience standing listening, and suddenly strode toward the pavilion to join the players. He picked up one of the spare guitars from among the extras standing there, plucked it a few times between numbers and then joined the band in their next few offerings. "Was he part of the group?" I wondered. Later I was told he was Claire Dodson, Daryl"s brother, partner in the now-defunct saw mill bearing the Dodson name.

I turned to the man next to me and asked, "When do you guys take the stand?"

"Two o'clock," he said. "If you like our music, come up to the Black Diamond Café next weekend; we play there every Saturday night."

"Where is that? I query.

"Up the mountain above Six Mile Run. You can't miss it; there's only one road. The action starts at six o'clock, and everything shuts down at ten o'clock."

I looked at my watch and sawee it was already one thirty. I glanced over toward the door of the dining hall and noted there were only three people in line, so I said, "Let's eat." Dottie was more than ready; the noon meal is important to her.

Inside the sweltering dining hall, we equipped ourselves with trays and fell in line. Carolyn Moseby, doing her community duty behind the counter, greeted us with her usual smile, and, at our order, plunked a half chicken and a roll on each of our plates. We grabbed dishes of baked beans and coleslaw from the dozens on the counter, and proceeded to the desserts, a table filled with a vast variety of pies; apple, cherry, peach, custard, lemon, chocolate. I grab a piece of apple pie, and the lady behind the counter said, "Ya want ice cream on it?" Naturally, I did. The cakes included double chocolate, which Dottie selecte in violation of her usual diet.

Serving at our next stop, the coffee and water table, was none other than Mike Purnell, the lay pastor of the Valley Methodist church. I grumbled a bit, mostly to myself, about the selling of bottled water when the local wells provide the best possible water. I balanced a cup of coffee on my tray and proceeded to the cashier's table, presided over by another of Ron's cousins, "Fiddle" Johnson, where Dottie had already had her tray of goodies totted up. I pay the tab, $3.50 for the chicken and roll; thirty-five cents apiece for the beans and coleslaw, fifty cents for ice cream and a quarter for my coffee, a little over ten bucks in all.

Across the table from us when we sat down was John Ford, the township supervisor and his wife Gladys, the regular church soloist. It was John who sparked the parade earlier in the day with his "Baby in the Wheelbarrow" act. People were constantly coming and going, and some with enormous bellies and/or posteriors were squeezing past us in the narrow space between the benches loaded with folks "stowing away the groceries." I feared at times, as these huge bodies pressed their way past me, that my face was going to be forced down into the coleslaw and beans on my plate.

A little after two, we regained our seats at the side of the band stand, where the Fulton Five were busily removing instruments and equipment, and the Black Diamond Miners were setting themselves up for their gig. It would be awhile before all the setting up, tuning up and loading up was finished.

A bit before two thirty, the Black Diamond Miners, boasting two guitars, a banjo, electric keyboard, drums and Uncle Jack with his violin, "let 'er rip" with "Red River Valley." The little boy with the guitar strummed aimlessly on his instrument. We listened with pleasure and clapped our hands after each number. Almost no one else applauded. The band continued with "golden oldies" like "Red River Valley," "Conin' 'Round the Mountain," "Wabash Cannon Ball" and "Hobo Bill."

After a time, Jim set his guitar down and helped the toothless Uncle Jack to his feet. They tottered toward the front of the stage, Jack with fiddle in hand, amid remarks from his colleagues, like "Keep your feet, Uncle Jack, you'll make it. Take yer time." The band members laughed, and the leader said, "Uncle Jack'll lead us in a few religious numbers." The old man lifted his fiddle, and backed by the band, sawed out "Amazing Grace," "This Is the Day the Lord Has Made" and "The Old Country Church," after which he tottered back to his seat, and the band continues, irreverently, with "I'd Love to Lay You Down" and "Windows Without Curtains."

The leader took a microphone to say, "The next number will be, 'She Broke My Heart, So I Broke Her Jaw'," and then quickly added, "Just kiddin', folks." There was a round of laughter among the listeners, and the musicians launched into "Black Mountain Ride."

We were tired, and, although we would have liked to hear more, decided to pick up an additional chicken half for our supper and head back to the shack. It had been a long but very pleasant day.

BLACK DIAMOND (21)
"What'll Ya Have?"

A week or so following the homecoming, after conferring with our friend Ron over a drink, we decided to investigate the Black Diamond Café and the entertainment recommended by The Black Diamond Six during the homecoming. Ron of course knew exactly where Six Mile Run is, and Dottie and I had gone to Sunday dinner there at the fire hall, but, none of us had ever heard of the Black Diamond Café or any other business or social activity there. Ron's impression was that for all practical purposes Six Mile Run was a ghost town with its few inhabitants either having chosen to live an isolated life, or possibly having been trapped there by the departure of all corporate mining efforts.

The decision having been made to visit the Black Diamond, we departed the shack on Saturday evening, with Ron driving the gray Chevie that had come into our lives as a result of the destruction of our two cars in Hurricane Frances. It was dark by time we got to Dudley, and it was then upward through the darkness, past a few house lights near the fire station at Six Mile Run, and then upward and onward to see what lay beyond. Finally, we sensed, or, possibly, could dimly see through the inky blackness, a few darkened houses on either side of the narrow road and concluded we were in or near our destination. The buildings seemed to front directly on the road. There was no light anywhere. Ron slowed the car to a crawl as we felt our way down the street. He finally remarked, "I don't think there is anybody in this place." Suddenly he swerved abruptly to the left to avoid running into the rear of a parked car, and we then proceeded to move even more slowly outboard of a number of cars parked along the road on our right.

Suddenly a blinding light cut through the black of night as someone either arrived or departed a building behind the parked cars. A blast of sound from the Black Diamond Pickers pierced the air. We concluded we had arrived at our destination. After picking our way through the intense black of the area, Ron struggled the car into the nearest available parking space, and we groped our way through the darkness to the door, once more blackened. When Ron opened the door there was again that burst of light and we were momentarily blinded. We stood at the entrance of an immense room in which several hundred people were seated at tables of various sizes mostly accommodating from two to eight seats each except for two huge tables just inside the door.

We just stood for a minute or two, allowing our eyes to adjust to the brilliant lighting. An older man wearing bib overalls, and sporting a grayish beard that flowed downward toward his waist, rose from a two-top table nearby and announced to us that he was leaving and we were welcome to his table. That was just as well, since there didn't seem to be any other vacancies in the place. Ron sauntered over to one of the large tables just inside the door occupied by a group of women hovering over a flock of young children ranging in ages from six months to ten years and borrowed an unused chair so we all could be seated.

The Pickers continued to beat out noisy renditions of the old country favorites. I caught the eye of my new-found friend, Jim Aller, strumming his guitar on the stage, thus reassuring him, I thought, that we had taken his invitation seriously and had risked our lives in the darkness to get there. I found myself wanting my usual pre-dinner cocktail.

Eventually, a gray haired woman, probably in her sixties, wearing a long flowered kitchen apron, appeared and inquired, as she wiped her hands on her apron, "Whadda ya want to drink?" I indicated that I'd like a martini, but plain gin on ice would do. The response was, "Coke, Seven Up, ginger ale, coffee or milk. No alcohol. Dinner is fried chicken or pork chop with potato and green beans. What'll ya have?"

Ron recovered his equanimity more rapidly than I, and said he'd like the chicken. Dottie concurred. Perhaps just to be different, I ordered the pork chop and coffee.

When the dinners were delivered a few minutes later, it was obvious that Ron and Dottie had out-ordered me. The chicken looked at least edible, and both recipients attacked their portions with vigor immediately. My pork chop looked like a piece of iron, and proved to be almost as resilient as iron during my attempts to eat it. It must have been on the stove since early afternoon. The greasy fried potatoes and green beans were almost as unappetizing. Looking around I noted that no such qualms were interfering with the dining experience of many of the others in the room.

When the Pickers' country music ended for their break time, any promise of silence was shattered with the blare of a recorded polka from the loud-speaking system. "Polka, everyone, pick your partners and take to the floor." Assorted couples complied: male/female; female/female, and even two male/male pairs stepped onto the floor. No one hooted, ridiculed or complained. Eventually these strenuous dances wore down most of the couples and the floor was empty.

The polka stopped abruptly and the voice announced, "Square dance time. Grab yer partner and Deau-Si-Deau. Here's yer favorite caller, Don Weaver, from Saxton!" A round of applause filled the room and square dance music flooded the arena. Numerous couples took to the floor, guided by the expert calling of Mr. Weaver, who turned out to be the man of many talents we had met at a Sunday fire house dinner a few weeks before. His talents, some of which also provided his livelihood, included auctioneering, selling used cars, breeding fox hounds, calling square dances and serving as a local constable and notary public.

We watched and listened for a few minutes, and then took Ron's suggestion that we leave before the exit rush that was sure to take place as the Black Diamond closed at nine thirty.

We found our car, mostly be feeling the fenders of cars en route, and then back through the blackness we went, with Ron expertly navigating the steep twisting road down the far side of the mountain. For a number of reasons, I was relieved that he was driving. He was familiar with the road, having driven it many times during his trucking career and then there was the fact that the newly black-topped road was not lined with the usual white so neither its edges nor its center line were visible in the intense darkness and thus indistinguishable from the surrounding terrain. All was black.

We finally passed through a series of sharp turns, passed a well-lighted house and arrived at an intersection with Wells Valley Road, less than a mile from The Shack.

It had been a great evening, and Dottie and I were happy to be home, but we have talked about that evening on many occasions that invariably conclude with the observation that we would like to do it all over again, but perhaps carrying flashlights.

COUNTRY LIVING (22)
Address It "Grandpa, Wells Tannery, PA."

Grandson Spencer, then about fifteen, received a check for fifty dollars as a birthday present from Dottie and me, as was our custom for the birthdays of all grandchildren, and now all great grandchildren, until such time as they reach adulthood and self sufficiency. More lately, as inflation has become an increasing problem, the birthday checks are written for a hundred bucks and the prospects are for even more inflation in the future. It's taxing to the old folks we have become, but it's good for our egos to be able to do this.

Spencer, not unlike other youngsters, was slow in writing any appreciation for the gift, but finally his mother, Martje, reminded him, "Grandpa's policy is if you don't express thanks for any gift he sends, it means you don't particularly like it and would prefer not to receive any similar gift in the future." Well, I couldn't have said it better myself. I have said similar things often, particularly to grandchildren.

By the time Spencer got around to writing his thank you note, spring had passed and Dottie and I were once again up at the shack in Wells Valley. House numbers had not yet been assigned in the valley, although they would be within a few years, partially as a help to give fire companies more exact locations for responses to fires. Mail was delivered, if at all, to Rural Route Box Numbers or Star Route Numbers. Much mail, including ours, was simply picked up at the post office from either a post office box or directly from the postmaster, Mary Lou Stiffel.

Spencer's letter of thanks finally arrived. In a large penciled scrawl the letter read, "Grandpa, Thanks for the Fifty Dollars. I bawt a GAMEBOY with it. Thanks, SPENCER." I was pleased to get some response and put Spencer back on my mental birthday list, but the big surprise to me came a little later, when I finally got around to looking at the face of the envelope that carried this impressive document. The address read "GRANDPA" on the first line and "WELLS TANNERY, PA 16691" on the second line.

Without hesitation Mary Lou, the postmaster had unerringly placed Spencer's letter with our mail to be picked up. She had simply looked at the postmark of Holland, Michigan and recalled that I had once mentioned I was a Dutchman from Holland Michigan. With the recall of that information she knew exactly how to deliver the missile. Now try that on a letter addressed in a similar manner to someone in New York City, Los Angeles, or even Holland!

Security is a community effort. For example, when big city burglars tried to get into the shack, knowing its locks were easily overcome, the Sharpes across the road called the constabulary, and then set off their own very loud warning system. The invaders left for fear they would be arrested, even though the area constabulary couldn't possibly get to the scene before the burglars had completed their ransacking of the house. Another law enforcement agency was the State police post seven treacherous winding road miles away up the mountain on US 30.

Fire is also a hazard that is constantly under surveillance by the neighbors. During the time I was clearing out the woods in the old potato field above the shack, my fires were regularly reported among the neighbors until I decided to just stack the brush and forget the fires, a better conservation process in any event.

Sharing is built into the country customs. During the growing season the bench at the post office holds a deposit of squashes, corn and other vegetables for use by any patron wanting them. On several occasions we were the recipients of vegetables, and on one occasion a gift of homemade bread from valley people we had not previously met.

It is true there is a little store in the village of Waterfall twelve miles away down the valley but it carries only a limited variety of foods and sundries in a space shared with the Waterfall post office. For a broader range of foods and other supplies one must travel either to the Fulton county seat at McConnelsburg about fifteen miles to the east after the trying climb over treacherous and winding State Road 915 to the top of the mountain or go west a similar distance to stores in the Everett-Bedford area. Although this situation is not always convenient, it does force one to adhere to carefully prepared lists of needs and desires before setting forth toward either of these destinations.

Bedford is a town with an extensive and colorful history. George Washington stayed there at least on one occasion during the Whiskey Rebellion; the Bedford Springs Hotel which stood in ruins during our time in the area is a mammoth wood framed structure that at one time rivaled Northern Michigan's Grand Hotel at Mackinac Island. We now have learned that this historic structure and its surroundings are undergoing extensive remodeling at a cost of many millions of dollars. In addition to the structures and renovation of the hotel grounds, the golf course has been completely torn up and rebuilt to the specifications of a well-known professional golfer.

The little city itself provides virtually all the amenities needed for a good life. First of all perhaps is the need for alcoholic beverages, and Bedford provides for this requirement with two separate outlets, one for beer and one for spirits in compliance with Pennsylvania's exotic liquor laws, which require this arrangement. The retail market is well served by stores both on Main Street and in outlying areas. A shopping area east of the city accommodates K-Mart a number of smaller retailers, and our favorite grocery store a Weiss market.

One of our all-time favorite restaurants is Ed's Steak House, an institution north of town providing a broad menu in two large dining rooms. Following an occasional Bedford shopping tour we stop at Ed's to enjoy the sizzler steak served on a hot platter in the cozy cocktail lounge with subdued canned music playing in the background.

A short distance down the road lies The Arena a similar "watering hole" favored by our friend, Ron Black and there the "music" is anything but canned. At least once a week Claire Dodson's brother Darryl and a few of his guitar plucking friends hammer out country music and provide a bit of humor with their antics. Others from among the winers and diners are invited to join them if they have come equipped with instruments expecting to be part of the scene. Guitars are the most common, but we have enjoyed music played on everything from a cross-cut saw to a saxophone with Darryl presiding over the whole in a manner mimicking the maestro of a symphony orchestra.

Fall festivals provide entertainment for thousands of people, many of whom travel hundreds of miles to participate in these events featuring many of the characteristics of country life. On static display are quilts, tractors of all ages and makes, horse driven hay rakes, old automobiles, steam driven threshing machines and a variety of other ancient items.

From time to time during the festivals the owner operates a cider mill powered by an ancient one-lung spark gap engine that grinds up apples, runs them through a press and spits out cider from one spout and pulp from another. Delicious cider is sold by the glass, the quart or the gallon. Much of the product of this press is sold on the spot to interested spectators, but not to Dottie; the apples used in the press often include wind dropped fruit and those that have become wormy. Seeing a wormy apple included in the feeding of the press she declined further cider. .

Each festival is opened with a Main Street Parade that includes an even larger conglomeration than at the Wells Tannery Homecoming. There are tractors, a collection of ancient steam powered farm machinery, bands, horses, automobiles, both old and new, and pretty girls hurling candy at appreciative onlookers together with entries from every church and organization in the area..

At each of the fairs we went to, there was plenty of country music, an abundance of food offerings, a number of antique stores, food booths and exhibits. As the programs state, "There is something for everyone."

At the Fulton affair the "Grease, Steam and Rust Association" displayed a collection of steam powered machinery owned by its members. Several of these ancient threshing machines and tractors kept in excellent operating condition were fired up periodically and operated by the owners. "Pulls" provided competition among a number of vehicles and we witnessed several of them. The Fulton Fall Folk Festival program of "Special Events" listed the following: Ford Pickup Pull; Antique Tractor Pull; Pedal Pull; Steam Engine Pull; Farm Stock Tractor Pull and Draft Horse Pull.

Streets were lined by shops displaying their goods al fresco and the antique shops were laden with actual antiques, bric-a-brac and souvenirs of current manufacture, many from overseas. Churches and school supporters did a land office business with their lunches, often served in the basement of the church or school.

In the summer across this entire scene falls the pleasant aroma of mew mown hay, the whining of the mowers, and upon both dawn and dusk the pleasant sound of innumerable birds singing their merry tunes. These relaxing and reassuring sounds are not duplicated in any city, except occasionally in a movie about those strange folks in the country.

BIRTHDAY PARTY (23)
"Flowers in Memory of Helen Knepper"

We had been gone for a couple of days to visit old friends in the Harrisburg area, but had returned late on Saturday, looking forward to the annual celebration of the birthday of Helen, the Knepper family matriarch, to be held the following afternoon. Helen would be ninety-three. Upwards of a hundred of her extended Moseby-Knepper family and friends would assemble on the expansive yard at the residence Rodney and Gail Knepper on Moseby Road. We were honored to be invited to join such a celebratory group.

We were seated in the church in our usual place toward the front of the sanctuary that Sunday morning as the rest of the tiny congregation assembled behind us. In the course of reading the announcements, the visiting lay minister said, "The beautiful floral arrangement in the front of the lectern were given by the Horton family in memory of Helen Knepper." We gasped in a mixture of astonishment and grief, and continued in that state of mind for the duration of the hour long service.

When we rose and turned around to greet the rest of the gathered worshippers, there was Helen, just as chipper as the previous week, looking forward to the celebration of her longevity that afternoon. The visiting minister had somehow substituted the word "memory" for "honor" or some other more appropriate descriptive term in inviting the attention of the congregation to the beautiful flower arrangement recognizing Helen's longevity. We drove home and devilled the dozen small eggs we had boiled before leaving for church, our contribution to the lavish presentation of food that would be displayed at Helen's party.

On our arrival at the Kneppers' just after the appointed hour of two, nearly a hundred people were already there munching on hamburgers, hot dogs, potato chips, potato salad, coleslaw, baked beans and dozens of other goodies. Smoke hovered above the barbeque grills presided over by Rodney and his brother, Steve, while Helen's daughters-in-law, Gail and Patti, bustled about to insure that everyone present was cared for and well fed.

Rod called out a greeting through the haze, "Are ya ready for a burger?" Naturally, we were; "Medium rare," I said, approaching the grill, "Those two right there will do if you get them off the grill right now."

"Nah," said Rod, "They're raw. Want cheese on 'em?"

"Take mine off. Put cheese on Dottie's, and then take it off too." Rod looked at me as though I were crazy. Perhaps we are, but that's the way we like our beef cooked. Wells Tannery folks don't think beef is done until it's dried out like shoe leather, but that is also their business. Under pressure, Rod took the burgers off the grill and flopped them on our opened buns, remarking, "You'll never grow old if we eat like that," ignoring the fact we were already almost as old as his mother.

Seven different kinds of cake, including one new to us, a speckled brown angel food cake made that way apparently by the introduction of brown sugar and chocolate chips in the otherwise standard mix. There were six pies ranging from my favorite apple to acustard, the latter not a favorite of either of us. We noted that the devilled eggs were already gone, so we picked up our empty egg tray and added it to the things on our table. I decided to wait to get my apple pie until after I had eaten the stuff on my plate, but by the time I went back for it, there was only a piece of crust left; it had a little thickened cinnamon and apple juice on it, so I grabbed this candy-like concoction with my fingers, gobbled it down with gusto, and left the plate completely empty. I licked my fingers before wiping them on a napkin.

Back at the table we were joined by Tim Moseby and his dear friend Lois Clark, and I was taught another thing about cuisine. Lois was munching on an ear of corn, "Good yellow corn, cooked just right," she remarked between bites. I had eaten an ear earlier and thought it mushy. I like white corn; she likes yellow. I like it to snap between my teeth; she likes it mushy, or creamy, or however one would describe what is, in my opinion, overcooked corn. Tastes do differ, of course. My Dad would have said, "Tastes differ said the lady as she kissed the cow."

Anyone who wanted to rode up the mountain in one of the three "Gators". Horseshoes were tossed. Baseballs were thrown around a trio out toward the road, and innumerable pictures were taken of Helen as she looked at the dozens of cards in a basket in front of her. Everyone was sated with food, and finally the guests started to depart, some with a hundred or more miles to drive. Dottie and I strolled over to the table at which Helen continued to preside, repeated our well wishes, and then made the rounds to thank Gail and Rodney and Steven and Pattie before returning to the shack. We had all eaten too much, but all have had a wonderful time at an important birthday party.

CASE REUNION IN RENO (24)
Coping With Death

Dottie had never really visited any place west of the Mississippi, with the exception of our brief visit to Las Vegas at Susan's invitation and our adventures in Hawaii and Calgary. On those occasions to get to our destination and return we flew over many of the western states without touching down. The opportunity, or perhaps our excuse, for traveling westward to California had its inception when I received the notice of the prospective annual reunion of Case sailors to be held in Reno, Nevada in August, but upon further reflection we discovered other reasons to go west.

My good friends from both college and navy days, Bill and Nola Van Oss, lived in Mountain View south of San Francisco had urged me, and more recently the two of us to visit them there in reciprocation for their many visits with Lory and me in the past. As our plans developed to attend the ship reunion in Reno, we found it easier and cheaper to fly from Pittsburgh to San Francisco rather than directly to Reno. This revelation naturally made me thinks that a combination of the visits in some way would be appropriate.

When I called Bill and Nola to see if this developing plan would be acceptable to them, their enthusiastic response was, "Please come and stay with us and use our place as a base for whatever else you want to do." I accepted with pleasure and expanded our plans to include several days of exposing Dottie to the wonders of San Francisco.

Our hosts greeted us as we deplaned at San Francisco International Airport and insisted that we go directly to their condo for an evening of rest and relaxation. "You can pick up the rental car in the morning," they said, and so it didn't take us much urging to agree, as we were already tired from a long day of traveling. It was a wonderful evening after a delicious dinner, and Bill, ever the raconteur, regaled us with stories of his adventures, those of his contemporaries and those of his ancestral lineage. There was no hint of the disaster that was looming in the lives of our hosts, but we went to bed realizing we had disrupted some of their sleeping arrangements.

We planned to get up fairly early in order to get down to the airport to pick up our rental car and get onward with our visiting San Francisco. Bill had always enjoyed his sleep, and so it was no surprise when we emerged from our assigned quarters, to find Nola in the kitchen assembling some things for breakfast. She greeted us with a cheery, "Hope you like peanut butter and sliced banana on wheat toast because that's what we're having. There is orange juice and coffee, or tea if you like." We explained Dottie's need to have herbal tea, and Nola responded that she had received some mint tea for Christmas, but had used none of it.

It was only after breakfast and the accompanying cheerful conversation during it that Nola invited us into the living room, lowered her voice, and said, "I just want you to know that Bill is dying." I think we reacted with a shocked silence. Nola continued, "He has an incurable wasting disease, and is not expected to live for more than few more weeks, perhaps a little more. We have accepted this and are doing our best to cope with it, although it's not easy. We are delighted you are here and hope you are comfortable. It's just that I wanted you to know that this might come to an end at any time."

After expressing our sorrow and best wishes to the extent possible under the circumstances, we suggested that we seek lodging somewhere else, but Nola was adamant, "Bill is happiest when he is with friends and Fritz is one of the oldest of them. Just go about your visit and we'll see you in the evening for dinner. "

We asked whether Bill would be able to go out to dinner and her response was, "Yes, there is a delightful little family restaurant just down the hill a ways and if Bill is able, it would be fun to go there." Reassured that we should continue our stay, we ventured off in our rental car and I enjoyed showing Dottie Seal

Rocks, some of San Francisco's western area, said to be where dope was prominent and thence to the Presidio where my Uncle Bill is buried and after visiting his grave it was onward to cross the Golden Gate Bridge and have lunch in a cozy little restaurant in the midst of the art offerings there. On the return trip we paused at the south end of the bridge to take in the view across the Golden Gate and to seaward. I related to Dottie that early in my naval career I had been the engineering officer of the *U.S.S. Case* when she collided in the fog with another destroyer, the *O'Brian*, and then we chose a different return route back to Mountain View to give Dottie the maximum exposure to San Francisco.

Dinner at the little restaurant down the hill was a pleasant affair, although Bill was tired, and said so. We didn't linger.

The next two days were occupied with visits to Chinatown, Market Street, Fisherman's Wharf, the top of the Mark Hopkins, several cable car rides and lunch at the waterfront, and then it was time for us to get to Reno and the *Case* reunion.

After the drive through the desert we were happy to get to the venerable Mapes Hotel and greet old friends, among them "Snuffy" Smith and his lovely wife. It was the last time I saw Snuffy, a shipmate who provided me with many a laugh as he related his always humorous naval experiences. He died before the next annual reunion. The ranks were thinning.

Another striking experience was when another attendee took my elbow and asked, "Don't you remember me?" I had to admit that I really didn't. He lowered his voice and moved to be away from any of our other shipmates and then said, "My name was Green. I cleaned your room and made up your bunk every morning for the two years you were in the *Case*. I was labeled as black then and so the only rate open to me was as a steward's mate, although I wanted to strike for gunner's mate. I don't think anyone else here recognizes me, but I thought you would."

It was an embarrassing confrontation and a reminder of how segregated the United States Navy was during World War II. He continued, "I'm a white man and am married to a wonderful white woman and have three wonderful white children. We have all the advantages that all of you have had all of your lives. I came to this reunion hoping I would see you. I don't think I'll attend any more *Case* reunions." All I could mumble in response was a heartfelt but inadequate, "I'm sorry."

Ship reunions, perhaps all unions of military and former military personnel, while most enjoyable, are also highly stereotyped. There is the hospitality room, there are the pre-arranged tours to "points of interest" and a banquet featuring a speaker who can relate to the interests of those in attendance. This one was no exception, and after three days we were on our way back to San Francisco.

When we arrived at the Van Oss condo, Nola informed us that Bill had returned to the hospital and the prognosis was that he would probably be dead within a few days. We suggested we stay elsewhere, but Nola insisted we stay for the two days until our scheduled departure.

When we visited Bill in the hospital it was obvious he had weakened in the few days of our absence. He strived to be his same old humorous self, but his jokes fell flat as he turned away to cough. It was a scene repeated daily all over the world, but it's different when the dying person is one to whom you are close. We flew home to Stuart and Bill died a few days later. Nola moved to New Hampshire to be near her son, an airline pilot.

PARTY TIME (25)
It Started Early and Ended Late

Whenever we were in Wells Valley we were entertained by a variety of people in various ways, provided regularly with welcome garden produce and assisted in innumerable ways. Not infrequently the sustenance came from people we had not known before.

A good example was a set of experiences we had with Raleigh Barnett the coal miner, mine owner and general entrepreneur whose career had been outlined for us by Ron Black some time before. Raleigh lived a mile or so up the valley in a rather secluded opening in the woods at the end of a lengthy driveway. We had once, in our explorations of the valley, driven back to his house not knowing where the narrow road was leading. We departed when we realized this was a private driveway. Thus we knew of him, but had never met him.

One afternoon as the corn silk was starting to turn brown in the fields, Raleigh appeared at the shack with three dozen ears of sweet corn in the largest of the brown paper bags used to bring home the groceries. "One dozen white corn, one dozen yellow corn and one dozen multi-colored corn. Tell me which you like and I'll bring you some more," he announced, one foot on the lower porch step with his thigh supporting the three bags. We invited him to join us on the porch, but he said, "No. I have corn to take to other folks before dinner, so I'd better get going."

When Ron came over to mow the meadow one time we asked him to tell us more about Raleigh, knowing that he knew "everything and everybody" in the valley. We already knew that Sandy Sharp across State Road 915 from the shack was Raleigh's daughter. Ron told us how her husband had been permanently injured in a trucking accident some years before while in Raleigh's employ; that Raleigh had an extensive collection of Fordson tractors and that he had a private picnic ground not far from the shack but well off the Valley road.

Raleigh dropped by and inquired which variety of corn we liked best, and we told him, "All of your corn is good, and picked when it's young and tender, but of the three we like the white corn best." Raleigh went back to his truck and carried a bushel of white corn up to the porch. We continued to eat corn for both lunch and dinner for the entire corn season.

We also felt obligated to the Moseby family who had often taken us into their family gatherings, including those on the Fourth of July, when we were fed glorious picnic food and after dark treated to extensive displays of fireworks. The Mosebys and others had included us in their progressive dinners and family gatherings. Steve and Rod Knepper included us to celebrate with them and their extended family the birthday of their mother as she approached her one hundredth year.

There were others, and so it was that we determined to have a party to include everyone in the Valley who wished to come together with a few from outside the valley to whom we sent individual invitations. We chose a date in August of the year which unbeknownst to us would be our last at the shack. We didn't go so far as to send out individual invitations to those in the Valley, but we did everything we could to let it be known that all would be welcome at the shack for an open house between the hours of one and five o'clock on the chosen Saturday. We posted an invitation on the bulletin board at the post office and asked the itinerant preacher to announce our open house to the congregation during the announcement period prior to the service on the two preceding Sundays, together with a request that the invitation be extended by those present to any and all in the Valley.

As the big day approached we faced a number of logistic problems forced upon us by the limitations of the shack. There was no freezer and the antiquated refrigerator was small with essentially no capacity to produce ice, so our ability to store foods needing refrigeration was extremely limited. Ron offered to help and was a great help throughout the preparation process and particularly as we moved toward the day of the event. Almost immediately in the planning process we gave up the idea of preparing our own potato salad and coleslaw, knowing that we could have it ordered for our pick up before the event from the market in Bedford.

When Raleigh became aware of our invitation, he offered what ever amount of corn we needed, so we asked him for a bushel of each of the three varieties he grew and he delivered the overflowing baskets in a just on time delivery the day before the event. We didn't have a kettle large enough to boil the quantities of corn we were going to need, so we followed an ancient American custom and borrowed a huge pot from the church. The electric stove in the kitchen had four burners, and two of these would be used for the corn.

Only frozen turkeys were available at the Weis store in Bedford, where we did our grocery shopping. We ordered two of the largest turkeys available, together with a twenty pound pre-cooked ham, twenty pounds each of potato salad and coleslaw, ten dozen potato rolls from the bakery and arranged to pick up the whole lot on Thursday so we could thaw the turkeys in the bath tub where they would be covered with water pumped up from the deep well by the wheezing old pump in the basement.

There was an electric crock pot and the home made beans we put in it were necessarily Bush's best spliced up with a bit of molasses, bacon and onions to give them some originality. We felt it necessary for a number of reasons to set up the self service table in the dining room of the shack just inside the front door from the screened porch. We turned the regular dining room table ninety degrees and installed the two leaves, so the table extended almost to the foot of the stairs and left just enough room between the table and the newel post so in case of need one could get to the "girls' bathroom."

With all this and more having been done, or at least planned, we faced up to a problem that had haunted us whenever we were in residence, the limitations of the electrical system. The building had been without electricity until it was purchased by Dottie's father and then wired piecemeal as additions were made over many years. There were two fuse boxes in the basement for two different circuits and each was labeled "20-WATT FUSES MAXIMUM." When 20-watt fuses were used, use of electricity was severely limited. For example, we couldn't brew coffee and cook pancakes on our griddle at the same time; they had to be separate operations. We had decided long since that 30-watt fuses should be installed, with close monitoring of the power being used. The kitchen stove and the water pump in the basement were wired for 220 volts, and were fused separately with modern wiring from the big transformer on a pole outside the house.

In summary, faced with all these power problems we cobbled up a tangle of extension cords borrowed from several different sources, temporarily put 40-watt fuses in the circuits and prayed for the best. The wires draped down the stairs from the bedrooms and underfoot from the great room and its relatively modern wiring system. We gave the system an hour long test on Friday afternoon and concluded it would last for the few hours of our party with only minimal risk we would burn down the shack. We could now keep the carvings from the turkey and ham warm, together with the gravy, rolls and beans.

There was no one-stop shopping for this event partially due the vagaries of Pennsylvania law and partially due to our own desire to make this a significant event in the valley. Isolation also played a part in creating the problems we faced. Early Thursday morning I set out to gather the materials needed from the areas to the west; Everett and Bedford. The first stop was at the state liquor store in Bedford to buy a bottle of Rebel Yell for Tim Moseby, who fancied himself a connoisseur of fine bourbons. We had decided not to serve spirits at our party, but Tim had always had a cocktail ready for us whenever we visited his place or attended his parties, no matter that the rest of the guests had to be satisfied with lemonade or soft drinks, so we felt obligated to reciprocate.

We made our way on the reverse course to stop at the Weis store for turkeys, ham, potato salad, coleslaw, stuffing bread, soft drinks, paper plates and cups, plastic tableware and all the rest.

In most jurisdictions outside of Pennsylvania one would normally buy all the alcoholic beverages needed or desired in one place. Not so in the keystone state where beer and spirits are by law sold from separate locations, so a stop at the state licensed beer store in Everett was a necessity. We had planned to buy four cases of Yuenglin, but as I talked to the manager of the beer sore he suggested that we buy a keg of Rolling Rock instead, "More beer for less money," was the way he put it, and then added, "For a few more bucks we'll deliver the beer and fifty pounds of ice; two twenty-five pound blocks right to your place." That sounded like a good deal to me, and I immediately accepted, as I worried he might balk when he realized where the beer was to be delivered. No matter; he took the location of the shack, acknowledged that he knew exactly where it was, and remarked, "We have to deliver a few cases to the store in Waterfall that day anyway."

Ever helpful Ron came over to the shack as soon as I returned and carried the potato salad and slaw over to his place for refrigeration. The two huge turkeys went into the bathtub and It was then a matter of adhering to a schedule such that all would be in readiness for the big event. I compromised my convictions somewhat on realizing that the first turkey might not be ready for stuffing by noon on Friday, so I started by filling the tub with warm water and let the frozen turkeys cool it off.

We tested our electrical layout for an hour with the 40-watt fuses temporarily in place and all of the appliances on full. The fuses didn't blow, and the house didn't burn down, although several of the long wire leads did get pretty hot. We judged the test to be a success.

Friday morning I cut five of the loaves of days old bread into one inch cubes, diced several pounds of onions and mixed the whole with sage and basil. At noon, I pulled the first turkey out of the bath tub and put it in the kitchen sink when I put my hand into the cavity at which point my fears were justified; the interior of the bird and the package of neck, gizzard, liver and heart were still frozen. I started a hot water treatment of the cavity and was eventually able to remove the package and proceed with the stuffing. Just a bit later than planned, the bird was in the oven and I could proceed with other preparations.

My plan called for the second bird to be stuffed late Friday evening and take the place of the first bird about one o'clock in the morning. I got a couple hours of sleep before the alarm aroused me to make the transfer and wrap the first bird in copious quantities of aluminum foil and brown paper to retain the heat.

It was a busy Saturday morning. Ron drove up to Breezewood to get a hundred pounds of bagged ice cubes. The beer truck arrived about ten, and the driver took a look at our bridge and decided it was too dangerous to cross; he didn't want a truck loaded with beer dropped into the creek. He wheeled the beer and ice up to the concrete slab outside the porch and tapped the keg for us. We put the keg in a wash tub surrounded by ice topped by cokes, root beer and orange pop.

Meanwhile, Dottie had put the ham on the griddle and sliced off a few pieces we could wrap into rolls for our lunch. We sat on the porch for a bit of relaxation after our strenuous efforts to get ready and speculated that if all went well, the party would be declared a success, the last of the guests would depart by five at the latest and we would be left to clean up the debris. Our speculation turned out to be a gross miscalculation.

It was about eleven when a car drove across the bridge up toward the house and parked. It was Harry Johnson and his lady friend who approached the shack. Harry, dressed in his cowboy dress-up outfit complete with ten gallon hat, high heeled boots and silver buckled belt, inquired, "Are we a bit early for the party?"

I wanted to reply, "You're two hours early, you are not welcome until one o'clock, so get lost until that time," but Dottie, ever the diplomat, said, "Draw yourselves a couple of beers from the keg, and come on up on the porch. Most of the food isn't ready, but I'll fix you a couple of ham sandwiches." So we sat and passed the time of day until Ron reappeared with the slaw and potato salad and they helped themselves at our invitation.

"Supposed to be in McConnelburg by early afternoon," our early birds remarked as they finished their repast, offered their thanks and departed. We ate our bit of ham sandwich, slaw and potato salad, and we got the rest of the repast on the table. The first turkey, wrapped in multiple layers of aluminum foil and brown paper was still quite warm when I put it on the hot plate, whacked off the wings and legs and carved a few slices of the breast.

Promptly at one o'clock John Ford in his battered pick up drove across the bridge and stopped. Gladys emerged carrying a pumpkin pie, but John stayed in the truck. "John thinks it's a church affair and he ain't comin' in. What time will the party be over?" We said it would be over at four as our announcements said it would be. "I'll go and tell John and he'll pick me up." It was clear that Gladys was there for the duration. I walked out to the truck with her. John was wearing one of the bib overalls he favored. I tried to persuade him to come up to the house for a sandwich, but he simply nodded the negative to me and then said to Gladys, "I'll pick you up at four; come across the bridge." He backed the truck across the bridge and rattled down the long driveway to SR915.

It was a good thing for John that he made his escape when he did or he would have been trapped by the cars and pick ups coming in through the lane. Our friends from Schellsburg, Hopewell, Bedford, Altoona and Six Mile Run arrived within minutes of each other and then a steady flow of arrivals from the community began. A few of the early arrivals interpreted our invitation as we intended, made a few sociable remarks, selected some food and made their departures, but it was clear that the remainder were there for the afternoon, and settled in all over the place, the old living room, the great room, the back porch, the screened porch and wherever they could find a place to perch. Many just stood and after having all the food they cared for, stood and drank either beer or coffee in considerable quantities. At one time I made a rough count and there were about a hundred people spread out across the premises. The overflow was now spreading out onto the meadow.

There was no need to worry about the carving of the meats; our visitors just whacked off what they felt like eating. I had thought the turkey legs and wings might be left on the platter, but early on I saw guests holding a wing or a drum stick gnawing away at these sometimes not favorite parts. By two-thirty I judged it was time to replenish the table with the second turkey, still in the oven, fill up the gravy pot with the last I had made and bring out the last of everything else we had put together for the party.

About then, the first of the Moseby clan arrived, Edith the matron, Bill and Caroline, their son and a couple of married cousins from New Jersey. Edith had baked a cherry pie and a blueberry pie and they were sliced and put at the end of the table with Gladys's pie next to the coffee pot and sheet cake.

Dottie mingled with the crowd and exchanged pleasantries. True to our agreement she did not participate in any of the serving or replenishing, but looked on with interest as I strived to cope with the inevitable problems and gave me a whimsical knowing smile once in awhile. The guests started to drift away, offered their thanks and departed to the sound of starting automobile engines.

We were down to about fifty stalwarts and I was picking my memory for the names of thos who hadn't come. Foremost were Pete and Pattie Ford, Fiddle Johnson and the young couple living on Blue Jay Lane with whom we felt wewanted to develop a stronger relationship.

We were looking forward to buttoning up the remnants, picking the carcasses of the turkeys, refrigerating what we could and get ready for a good night's sleep.

It was then that the party began. Tim and his friend Lois Clark arrived, followed by two cars loaded with some of their friends, two of whom came equipped with guitars. I made a ceremonial presentation of the bottle of Rebel Yell, which Tim promptly opened, stripping the wax seal off with his jackknife as he announced that everyone else could drink beer, but he was going to enjoy his present. After everyone had sampled the alcoholic beverages, they tackled the remnants of the food and pretty much cleaned up what was left on the makeshift table.

Edith and the rest of the Mosebys as well as a large share of those who had stayed to the designated end of the party said their adieus and left. It started to get dark and the guitars started to play some of the old country songs that everybody knew, sprinkled in with some popular music that only the younger set knew. It was fun, but I had had enough; I was tired through and through. Lois finally tugged on Tim's sleeve and said something like, "Come on big boy the party's over and it's time to go," with that she and Tim slithered off into the dark followed by the rest of balladeers. We barely made it to church on Sunday morning.

KIRK REUNIONS (26)
We Meet Valerie and Other Cousins

Keith Kirk was the owner of a Ford dealership in Hancock, Maryland and lived with his second wife, a young child and a dog on a sizeable piece of heavily rolling partially wooded land near the town of Needmore, about fifty miles south of the shack. Once, early in our marriage as we were passing Needmore Dottie remarked, "This is where one of my shirttail cousins lives. He's a prosperous car dealer in Hagerstown named Keith Kirk."

Not long thereafter, Dottie received an invitation to attend te seventy-fifth annual Kirk family reunion to be held at the home of Keith Kirk. Enclosed with the invitation were detailed instructions on how to drive to the site and a listing of what potluck items would be appropriate for the occasion. As she crumpled the invitation in her hand in preparation for throwing it in the trash, Dottie said. "I went to one of those reunions with my grandparents one summer when I was a little girl and visiting them in the valley. I get these invitations every year, but I only know a few of the people who might attend, a bunch of second and third cousins, a bevy of children and a group of old folks sitting in the shade. The few I do know are getting older each year, as I am and I'm not sure they would even recognize me."

I said, "Whoa, honey. Don't throw that away; it might be fun to attend and meet all those folks who are your kith and kin." With some reluctance she spread the invitation and the directions accompanying it on the table and we did look at them critically. The result was we did attend; it was the first of five such celebrations in which we participated, and after those years I seemed to be accepted as a member of the clan, since my wife was a Kirk.

Somehow I had pictured in my mind that perhaps twenty or thirty people might be attending the first reunion in which we participated, but after driving up the long single lane private drive leading up to the massive Kirk house at the top of a hill, I was disabused of this notion when, at the end of the climb we arrived at the back of the manor looking for a parking place among the hundred or more cars of all makes and models, some new, some old congregated there.

We were lead by the sounds of animated conversations to take a route around the outside of the four stall garage at the end of the massive brick house, and were shortly surrounded by Kirks of all ages, sexes and occupations. A large ruddy-faced blond man strode toward us as we rounded the end of the garage. "I'm Keith Kirk. Welcome to the reunion." Dottie had refreshed her memory of how the various Kirks of her grandfather's branch of the clan were related, and gave Keith a couple of sentences that identified her as one of his first cousins, twice removed.

A beautiful youngish woman, perhaps half Keith's age, approached and was introduced as Keith's wife. She led me to the kitchen where I deposited the iron pot of baked beans we had carried with us as our contribution to the forthcoming repast. It was only later that in conversation with several of the more knowledgeable attendees we learned that Mrs. Keith Kirk was the second to hold that title and that she was the mother of a beautiful young girl who flittered around through the crowd. We were also informed that two of the children from Keith's first marriage were busily playing games with other young people.

Keith had arranged for a huge tent to be set up on the lawn to shelter the extended Kirk family from the sun, or possible rain. The expansive tent was similar to the one under which the auctioneer at the earlier Baumgartner auction had performed his functions. At one end of the tent sat an obviously crippled man in a wheelchair with a board across his lap for use as a desk. He was informally taking the roll of those present and seeking to record the vital statistics on people new to the annual event. This was Noah Linn Hendershot, secretary of the loosely organized Kirk Reunion Group and it was to this gentleman that Dottie presented her credentials as a Kirk.

We later met Dottie's second cousins, Valerie Hachtel and Mary Weaver, who were also attending the reunion for the first time. Mary and her husband took seats on a bench in the tent and didn't move until the meal was served, but Valerie, whose husband Buddy was not present, spent the time flitting about through the crowd, making her presence known to all.

At about one o'clock a huge bell, probably retrieved from a country school house that was being razed, was sounded as a signal for all to assemble for the picnic lunch. There was a prayer by a Kirk Presbyterian clergyman, and the feast began. We had a fine time, enjoyed the food and on the drive home commented to each other on the evidence that the Kirks were not only a cohesive group, but also on how impressed we were with the apparent financial success of all, and particularly the apparent wealth of our host.

Our second Kirk reunion a year later was a mirrored image of the first plus a few added attractions. A pond had been dug on the hillside a short distance from the mansion. It was lined with plastic to prevent leakage into the sandy soil. A small raft floated in the center of the pond and we were informed that the pond had been stocked with bluegills and bass. A small herd of goats had been installed on the premises to cut the grass on the slopes beneath the mansion and control the spread of unwanted trees and bushes by eating them before they became too large.

Our ebullient host and his young wife were perfect images of hospitality. There was every indication that Keith was enjoying continued success in the car business. We left sharing comments similar to those we made after our first reunion.

For reasons we didn't understand at the time, the following reunion was held at the city park in Hagerstown, Maryland, a beautiful site filled with walking trails wooded areas and recreational facilities, plus a large shelter built to house large groups for picnics, family reunions and other summertime gatherings. I took note of the absence of our previous hosts, but assumed they had other responsibilities conflicting with the family reunion. The standard format was followed, and after the lunch, among other prizes made was one for "the oldest Kirk present" awarded to a woman in her nineties from another branch of the family. In accepting the award for the Kirk who had traveled the farthest to attend, Dottie commented, "I am the second oldest Kirk here today, but I don't want that award any time soon,"

When we received our invitation to the next reunion the site had been changed to a community center in Worfordsburg. The affair would be held indoors as there were no suitable outdoor facilities. The directions to the community center were very carefully written, and we followed them exactly, but when we arrived at the site there was only one car there. I walked around the building to see whether there were any indications of where we should go. We waited until noon and by then several other cars had driven up. We consulted among us, but no one had any suggestions for what we should do.

A few minutes later, another car arrived, and its driver had been dispatched to round up any would be participants who had gone astray. Apparently the change of venue had been posted at the entrances to the community hall, but had disappeared, perhaps blown away. The new site would be the recreation building attached to the Presbyterian church of Worfordsburg.

The space available in the building was not adequate for the group already assembled there, and with the addition of our group of strays the recreation center was grossly overcrowded, but having no alternatives, the reunion went off as scheduled, albeit with participants occupying the several connecting rooms in the building. After delivering our food contribution, a large bucket of potato salad, Dottie and I were assigned to one of those adjoining rooms and found ourselves seated with Keith Kirk. We exchanged a few pleasantries and asked about his wife. He responded somewhat circuitously, and then a bit ingenuously I inquired, "How is business?"

He responded, "Not good. I lost the Ford franchise, and now I'm trying to sell cars, both new and used, for a former competitor.

Continuing with my naiveté I inquired, "What about your house? Are you still living there?"

"Yes," he said, "But I don't own it. The bank has allowed me to stay in the house as long as I maintain it and pay the electric bill. As soon as they sell the place, which they certainly will do soon, if only to rerieve their equity, I will have to vacate immediately." He then added, "But I'm getting along OK." I didn't have the temerity to inquire into the whereabouts of his family members.

After dinner and the various awards had been made, Dottie rose and entered the main hall to speak to all within earshot. "I have compiled a genealogy of the Kirks on my side of the family as far back as I have it. The first entry is for a Jack Bowers who was born in the early seventeen hundreds. The Kirk name appears when my great-great grandfather James Kirk, married a Jane, but I do not have her maiden name, My grandfather had twelve sons, and thus the work is fairly large, but if you would like to have a copy I will mail it to you." Eight or ten hands rose in the room and Dottie prepared to circulate a tablet for those folks to inscribe their names and addresses, but was interrupted when Linn Hendershot spoke from his wheelchair and suggested the document be duplicated there in the church office. The cousin who had arranged for use of the building appeared with the necessary key and copies were made and distributed to all interested parties.

After the dinner, awards were made in various categories such as the oldest Kirk in attendance, the youngest, various other categories and finally one for the Kirk who had traveled the farthest to attend. Dottie won the award for distance traveled, but in accepting her award she took note of the fact she was the runner up for the first category, but not anxious to receive the prize. Linn's mother, Evelyn V. Kirk Hendershot had received that one.

The next two reunions, the last we were able to attend, were held at the Hagerstown City Park, where a beautiful roofed picnic area was ample to shelter the all the Kirk clan who were in attendance. The parking area was adequate for the parking of a large number of vehicles, but it was a long, uphill struggle for us to get from there to the shelter, carrying our basket of equipments and the five pounds of potato salad we had purchased as our contribution to the picnic meal. We were pretty well tuckered out by the time we got to the shelter and found a place to sit.

Following the opening prayer the group of about a hundred bantered and ate of the ample variety and amount of foods contributed until all were well sated when our attention was invited to a man carrying a bagpipe and wearing entirely Scottish garb, from stockings and a kilt to the tam on head. He played a considerable number of Scottish tunes with the raucous sounds of the pipes. Later someone remarked, "We should have him play for us at every reunion."

The immediate response from Linn Hendershot, the treasurer, was. "We can't afford him. One of our clan paid for his performance today, but we can't do that every year." Linn's remark reflected the fact that the only funds possessed by the clan were obtained by dues of two dollars for each person present, collected by passing an empty lard buckrt along the tables.

How we managed to attend all the parties and picnics, all the Rotary affairs, all the reunions we did is something of a mystery in retrospect. One that comes to mind is our visit to the home of Valarie Hachtel, Dottie's second cousin twice removed, and her husband Buddy. The couple lived on Merritt Island, in a modest house facing one of the many waterways intersecting that area with their thirty-foot power cruiser moored at their private dock in the back yard. We wandered around through the roads or streets forced by the waterways into their contours.

By the time we arrived at the Hachtel's place, it was almost noon that Sunday, and we had been there only a short time there when they announced, "We have planned to have lunch on the boat, and it's about a half hour from here at the low speed we have to maintain on these waters to our favorite secluded bay." It was almost two o'clock by the time we got to our destination and dropped the anchor.

Valerie had packed a great luncheon basket and we enjoyed our loll in their cockpit partially shaded from the sun so I could enjoy the warmth while Dottie stayed out from the rays that are her nemesis. It was a delightful afternoon with our new-found cousins.

Buddy was already retired, but Valerie still worked as the occupant of the front desk and telephone operator at an assisted living establishment, and she thus had to leave in the morning. Dottie, having been an inspector of such places asked if she could ride along and informally inspect the operation, as she planned to write a book on the subject of homes for the elderly when she found the time in our busy schedule. Valerie was most agreeable and offered to drive Dottie back during her lunch break so we could start on our trek home. My morning was spent enjoying a cigar in the sun while Buddy sanded an revarnished some of the bright work on their boat.

It had been a pleasant two days with second cousins we had met in person only once before. Buddy died a year or so later, and now we exchange Christmas cards with Valerie, the whole scene characteristic of life among the elderly.

MORE REUNIONS (27)
"Old Sailors Never Die..."

Intertwined with the rest of our activities were the reunions of the *U.S.S. CASE* crew scheduled for various geographical locations across the country in an attempt to equalize, at least to some degree, the amount of travel required over the years. One of these held in Reno, Nevada, has been described previously. The social characteristics of the reunions were fairly uniform over the years, with a hospitality room arranged in the host hotel, a tour or two of the area's attractions and a banquet as a finale. Below is a listing of those events and a few brief descriptions or comments as I recall them.

SAN DIEGO

We had just nicely gotten settled in our new apartment in Hanson's Landing following our move from Pierpointe Yacht Club when I received a call from an old friend and shipmate in the U.S.CASE informing me that a group of former crewmen living in Southern California had gotten together to organize a ship reunion with the first to be in San Diego. I announced this good news to Lory, expecting an enthusiastic favorable response to the invitation for me to join old shipmates, even if she would only know the Ramages, Don and Helen. Don had been one of my mentors in the CASE and we two couples had had a number of opportunities to be together over the years. I was crestfallen when she responded, "I'm not going; you can go if you want to."

I went, but with a heavy heart. It was great to be with old friends and I even enjoyed being thrown fully clad into the motel swimming pool by a couple of my former engineers. After hearing my enthusiastic report of the reunion, Lory agreed to attend all future reunions, and she did until no longer able to do so.

NORFOLK

Our gathering in Norfolk was highlighted by a tour of the *U.S.S. COMTE DE GRASSE* arranged by my son, Fred III, who was at that lime a lieutenant commander and the executive officer of the ship. She was the latest in destroyer design at that time, and more than three times the displacement of the *CASE,* with a crew about a third that of the earlier ship aboard which we were all shipmates.

Buck, as we called our son, gave us a guided tour of the ship taking us into virtually every part of the ship except for the bilges and one or two highly classified areas. At each significant area the petty office in charge gave us full descriptions of the functions and significance of what took place there during operations. Our group was impressed by the developments that had occurred since were operating many years before during World War II, and the young sailors of the crew were proud to show off their ship to a bunch of ancient mariners.

SAN DIEGO II

After Lory's death there was another occasion during which we took advantage of "space available" housing in bachelor officers' quarters, although our stay was not without some moving around, circumstances made easier by the fact that on our arrival we had rented a car for the duration of our stay. We requested quarters at the Naval Air Station, San Diego, commonly referred to as "North Island" for the entire eight day period we were planning to stay, but commitments to higher priority requests put us into quarters at the Naval Station, San Diego, across the bay from the air station, making a move necessary in the middle of our stay.

All of this was familiar territory to me, as I had had several tours of duty based on the San Diego area and we had lived in Coronad, just four blocks from the air station main gate. I took the opportunity during out days at North Island to show Dottie my former haunts in Coronado and the air station. Fortunately, one of the fleet carriers was alongside the pier and was open for ship visits, and we took full advantage of the guided tour.

We made a quick stop at the building that had housed the offices of Fleet Air Wing Fourteen, where I had served as ship training officer, and verified what I already knew, that seaplanes were no longer operational in the fleet, and then it was on to the Navy Exchange for a few purchases.

In Coronado we drove down to the old ferry dock area, now a city park, at a taco at the *Mexican Village* drove around to see the block of rental properties I had once owned, and then, finally, stopped at the beautiful little two-bedroom house at 365 "H" Avenue where Lory and I had lived off and on during the mid-career years of my naval service. It was a nostalgic stop for me.

I parked our rental car in the driveway and noted that the garage was no longer a garage, but had been converted into a room with a beautiful window and flower vox where the garage door had been during out occupancy. I couldn't resist going up to the door and pressing the bell. The owner, as middle aged lady responded and invited us to tour the house with her. With the exception of the garage, everything seemed the same as when we had left twenty years before.

The patio I had laid adjacent to the house was now covered with a canopy as a shield from the sun and rain, but three of the concrete blocks still had molded in them the footprints of the three children of our family at the time we lived there. "I have often wondered how those footprints got there, and now I know, declared the lady of the house.

The reunion itself was in the standard pattern, highlighted by a visit to Old Town San Diego and great visits with shipmates.

SAN ANTONIO

This was more of the same, but with a different flavor, the boat ride on the canal being the high light event. I attempted to contact old friends living there, but without success.

BRANSON

We decided to drive to Branson, Missouri, a self-propelled show town with no gambling, from our home in Stuart, a distance of almost two thousand miles, partly because air travel to that show town was difficult, involving several changes of planes, and finally a landing fifty miles from the place. We took our time driving reasonable distances to get there, stopping overnight on a Mississippi gambling boat, and later on the edge of the vast woodlands prior to getting to our destination.

Our committee had planned for the *CASE* group to see a show each of the four evenings we were there, including a comedy, a country music show and the one man performance of a very funny "Mad Russian."

SOUTH DAKOTA

There was much friendly banter among the former *CASE* sailors when Rapid City, South Dakota was selected as the site for what turned out to be the 2003 reunion of the ship's company. Charles Kayl stood at our Branson meeting and said, "If you will come to Rapid City, my wife will make all the plans and arrangements and you'll have a good time. There is plenty of good stuff to see in the general area of Rapid City."

One of our members at the meeting said, "Let's visit your ranch. That would be a great experience for all of us."

Our prospective host shot back, "We'd be delighted to have you, but keep in mind that our place is three hundred miles east of Rapid City, we live in a five bedroom house, so we can only accommodate a few of you there; the nearest restaurant is twenty-five miles away and the nearest motel or hotel is nearly a hundred miles away. You figure out the arrangements and we'll be happy to host the group for a visit." Following a roar of laughter that suggestion was quickly dropped, but it did impress on many of us the vastness of South Dakota.

Charlie was true to his word; his wife did all the work and we did see a lot of interesting things. The Badlands, Little Big Horn and an evening visit to Mount Rushmore were among the many attractions we visited on the first of several tours involving lengthy trips by bus. On a second tour we visited Deadwood, Spearfish Canyon and the Homestake Mine area. It was a great visit with old friends and shipmates, and at the farewell banquet, the group voted unanimously to hold the next reunion in the Washington, D.C. area.

WASHINGTON, D.C.

Our actual headquarters hotel for this reunion was The Hilton in Arlington, Virginia where we took advantage of the many historic sites, including the Viet Nam Memorial and Arlington National Cemetery, where I paid a visit to the crypt where the ashes of my late wife are entombed and where mine will be placed following my death. A highlight was our visit to the newly completed World War II National Memorial.

As a group we visited the U. S. Navy Memorial in downtown Washington, where we were honored with a tour of the museum, a special showing of the navy film, "At Sea," and a memorial service honoring our deceased *CASE* veterans. As the senior member of the group, and as a memento of the occasion I was given a bronze plaque molded in their building yard depicting silhouettes the *CASE* and *U. S. S. CONYNGHAM (DD371).*

I mounted the plaque on a piece of varnished hardwood and hung it in our den among the cherished reminders of my life where I see it every day and often give thought to whether any one or any institution would be interested in it after my death. There will probably never be another *CASE* (she was named after a Civil War officer commanding groups of ships during the blockade of the South) and the name of the *Conyngham* is not likely to appear on lists of navy ships in the future either.

As various members of our group wanted to visit other Washington sites, we devoted a day to those activities. At the farewell banquet, which turned out to be our last, we voted to return to California the next year if our proposed host, Wayne McClure, a resident of the valley, could make the arrangements in the Napa Valley for a total price these retirees could afford.

+NAPA VALLEY FINALE

It was not to be. Our proposed host for the next year's reunion, Wayne McClure, found that there were no accommodations to fill our needs, even in the off-season; everything was booked. Several attempts were made by mail and e-mail to settle on a date and place for another reunion. All failed. Finally, after caucusing the members, it was decided to give the treasury of the *CASE* survivors, amounting to $2,222.11, to the Navy-Marine Corps Relief Society, an organization that had helped several of our crew through the financial difficulties resulting from our not being paid for the first six months of United States participation in World War II.

In retrospect one would think it impossible to squeeze into our lives as many activities as we did during the few years we still had the health and strength to travel to, and participate in the activities of Rotary, family, ship reunions. Rotary alone engaged much of our attention. Dottie became a Rotarian and we attended District Conferences, Zone Institutes, meetings of past district governors and their spouses as well as national conventions in Chicago, San Antonio, Mexico City, Calgary and Portland, Oregon.

One particularly memorable Rotary Zone Institute was held at the Grand Hotel on Mackinac Island, and we took full advantage of the time between sessions to take carriage ride around the island and do a bit of shopping.

There also were the fall festivals held each year in Bedford and Fulton counties, with the major activities and exhibits centered in the cities of Bedford and McConnelburg, the county seats. There actually were three weeks of festivals with one week in October dedicated to the Fulton Fall Folk Festival and the week on either side assigned to the Bedford affair. At Dottie's insistence we attended several of these events, inviting one or more couples among her cousins to join us.

TIM'S PARTIES (28)
We Receive Special Treatment

We were just summer visitors to Wells Valley and not really a part of the community, although everyone treated us with kindness and consideration. In particular, the extended Moseby family extended their friendship and hospitality to us well beyond what might be expected under the circumstances. On several occasions Edith Moseby included us in family affairs to which we could not realistically expect to be invited. On several occasions we were included in Moseby family Fourth of July celebrations that lasted until the last sky bomb and Roman candle had been fired. On many occasions Edith invited us after church to share a bit of pie and ice cream with her and we enjoyed her company and the stories of what the valley was like before electric power was brought in during the depression. There was a similar relationship with Bill and Carolyn Moseby and with the Kneppers, whose matron had been born a Moseby.

I was intrigued by the fact that Bill and Carolyn were retired from the Central Intelligence Agency after serving many years in Africa on assignments there. One might have expected them to retirement to live in a more cosmopolitan community, but their choice was to return to Wells Valley and share in community leadership, while Bill enjoyed the role of gentleman farmer.

Edith's daughter, Rosemary and her husband, Ward Woodall, both CIA retirees, chose to live in a subdivision in West Virginia, an easy commute to Wells Tannery for regular supportive visits with her mother.

Bill's younger brother, Tim chose a different direction when he graduated from Rollins College, as had Bill. Intensely interested in agriculture, Tim chose to combine farming with establishing retail outlets for John Deere agricultural equipment at two locations in Central Pennsylvania, some distance from his personal home base in the valley.

Once each year Tim hosted an afternoon potluck picnic at his home in the valley on a Sunday September afternoon for all of the employees at his John Deere locations, together with their families, plus his extended family and a limited group of others among which for several years we were fortunate enough to be included. Tim made his home on one of his several farms in the valley, just to the east of Moseby Road

Tim's farm house, barn and machinery shed were on a rise off Metzler Road just a few hundred feet east of its intersection with Moseby Road. Unfortunately, due to intervening health problems Dottie and I encountered during the following half year this was destined to be our last summer in the valley and thus the last of a number of Tim's parties we attended. The format was always the same but the afternoon was always a pleasant one. Because most in attendance had to drive a considerable distance, while the arrivals were planned to be at noon, the actual arrivals were usually spread out over about an hour from eleven thirty to twelve thirty. Counting on that pattern we planned to arrive about one o'clock carrying our platter of devilled eggs as our contribution to the potluck aspect of the affair.

Most of Tim's extensive collection of brand new John Deere machinery was always on display at various locations on the premises for this affair and the modern machinery shed was kept empty for the day as a shelter in case of rain. The barn, about half full of baled straw, was not so modern. In fact, it was probably the oldest building on the farm. Six long tables, several improvised from the straw bales with panels of some kind as tops, were arrayed in the open part of the barn to provide seating for at least a portion of the guests.

There also were several picnic tables set up in an array on the lawn outside the house to accommodate the assortment of devilled eggs, vegetable platters, green salads, potato salads, assorted gelatin dishes, coleslaws, vegetable dishes and pies, cakes, brownies and many other delicious dessert concoctions with identifying names such as "Aunt Betty's Peanut Butter-

Banana Brownies" and " Terri's Tasty Toffee." One card table was reserved exclusively for pickles and preserves; another for a great variety of delicious home made breads. Packed in ice were tubes containing several varieties of Cousin Rodney's home made ice cream including one locally famous variety named for one of its principal ingredients, Grape Nuts.

As we arrived we noted several grills already fully ablaze set up on the driveway outside the barn with, in our opinion, far too much charcoal, ready to insure that every piece of steak would be well done to the point of ruination. There was much jesting as we arrived concerning the fact that we would prefer our steaks medium rare, or as one of the appointed grill masters referred to our preference, "Raw. Why dontcha just whack a piece offa one a them cows over there and eat it?" waving a hand toward one of the neighbors' cows grazing peacefully in a field. We knew that Tim had reserved a couple of steaks to be grilled for us somewhat later when we hoped the fires would have died down somewhat. Tim, however, was nowhere to be seen.

Several John Deere Gators were moving up and down the nearby slopes, and across the mowed fields across the road, with cargos of children shouting and laughing.

We slithered about through the crowd, renewing old acquaintances and meeting new ones who advised us on the weather, the crops and whatever else was going on their lives. Edith arrived, having been picked up by Bill and Carolyn, and took a seat in the barn near the door, a position that gave her nearly a full view of what was going on in the gravelled area surrounded by house, the tool shed and the barn. Daughter Rosemary and her husband, Ward Woodall, were not far behind and Rosemary assumed her position as guardian and caretaker for Edith.

Two ladies serving as Tim's assistants came down the walk from the house and across the gravelled area carrying two tremendous platters of strip steaks for deposit on small tables near the grills. The team of men designated to grill the steaks filled all the grills to capacity over the intensely hot charcoal, and immediately a plume of smoke ascended from the grills and the smell of burning flesh filled the air while the steaks were charred to a crisp. "Just right," declared one of the grillers as a few guests, plates in hand filled with their other choices, arrived to claim a steak apiece and the process continued. One of the men, seeing us nearby called over, "Don't worry, we'll have your steaks here when you want to cook 'em."

We decided it was time to go up to the house and deliver Tim's bottle of Rebel Yell. He saw us coming and held the door open. "I just poured you a couple of your favorite beverages. Join me." On the kitchen counter top was an array of alcoholic beverages, reserved for privileged guests such as we were, together with a bucket of ice and two glasses for us charged with vodka for Dottie and bourbon for me. We hoisted our glasses with Tim and passed the time of day for a time as we stood in his kitchen. Finally, he said, "Well I'd better go out and greet everybody," and headed for the door. We followed and since everyone else at the party was eating we felt we should grill our steaks, even though the grills were still glowing with red hot charcoal. Amidst much jesting and laughter, we cooked our steaks medium rare and joined the Moseby group in the barn to enjoy our delicious meal.

An hour or so later Tim corralled a couple of the younger men and went up to the house and returned carrying enough shotguns and ammunition to equip a squad or two of soldiers for a small war. With some more male help a couple of boxes of clay pigeons and two mechanical devices to throw them were carried to a high point beyond the machinery shed and set up on the turf. Everyone was invited to shoot, although only one or two of the women did.

Every standard gauge of shotgun was available and both traps were in use as the call of "Pull," reverberated between the sounds of firing. Young boys fired the .410 gauge guns while older folks fired the larger gauges. Two women took their turns and one of them made a better showing than most of the men. I tried my hand for a few shots, but found that my strength was waning such that I could hardly hold a gun up to my shoulder.

As the sun dipped down below the tops of the trees the sounds of engines starting were commingled with farewell comments as the assembly of cars and pick ups disbursed. It had been a wonderful afternoon with a group of wonderful down to earth people.

A week or two later, Dottie was included in a shopping expedition to Bedford with Rosemary and Edith, Tim's sister and mother, respectively. Upon their departure, Tim arrived at the shack driving his John Deere Gator utility vehicle shortly after the ladies had left and called out, "Come on, Fritz, we're going for a ride." I had no idea what he had in mind, but it seemed like a good way to pass a part of the day. I climbed on board the two-seater and we proceeded down the lower trail along the creek that paralleled for a distance the upper trail which led to where I had worked for a number of years pruning the trees and clearing undergrowth on a ten acre plot of ground that Dottie had had planted with spruce, white pine and linden.

Our route was rough, even though I had put in some time trying to move some rock and earth by hand to attenuate some of the more bump-ridden lengths of the trail. We followed the creek around to where it ran under Metzler Road and made a left turn on the black top past the house where Tim's friend, Lois Clark had tried without success to start a bed and breakfast establishment for horse lovers, and thence past the end of the pavement to another farm yard that Tim informed me was also hers.

Tim had talked constantly on this first leg of our adventure as he described everything we passed, crops, animals, tree varieties, flow of the creek and lay of the land. We stopped at the barn, and Tim reached into a bag in the cargo bin of the vehicle and pulled out two half pints of Rebel Yell. "One for you and one for me," he proclaimed, "Have a drink." It was late morning, much earlier than I would normally even think of having a drink, but I was his guest, and I thought it would be impolite to refuse, so I took what I thought might be an appropriate sip of the beverage. Tim disagreed. "Naw, have a decent drink," he urged and I complied.

"Lois lives here some of the time," said Tim and he reminded me that the house has five bedrooms and four baths. Dottie and I had attended a party there several years before and had been invited to take a tour of the huge house now occupied part time by one person. We drove a mile or so further, inspecting her mixed herd of beef cattle, horses and goats, before turning around to retrace our route back to the bottom of the hill. "Better refresh ourselves for the climb up the hill," said Tim, taking a pull from his bottle and urging me to do the same.

We drove to the top of the wooded hill and Tim stopped at a fence line of barbed wire. Looking across the fence was an open field of sprouting wheat. "I own that forty, and Lois owns the next one." He took another pull from his bottle and I took a sip from mine, and then we drove to the boundary between Tim's and Dottie's land, where a huge oak had blown over across the dividing barbed wire fence.

We drove past all the areas where I had planted young trees and inspected several rows of those I had pruned, all at rather high speed, weaving between trees in areas where the spacing of the planted trees was barely more than the width of the vehicle in which we were riding. "Whee Haw," shouted Tim as we raced down the rows of trees, "We're having fun." I wasn't too sure.

"Now I'm going to show you the most beautiful spot in Fulton County. We went down the trail to the shack, where Tim felt inclined to have another sip of Rebel Yell and then it was down the road to State Road 915, up Moseby Road and back to his house, where we stopped only briefly before passing between the barn and the machinery shed, past the site where a few weeks before had been the cannonade and clay pigeon shoot, and entered a track that led to the top of the ridge, where Tim stopped abruptly at the edge of an escarpment overlooking a broad expanse of Fulton and Bedford Counties. "Where could you find a more beautiful place than this? He asked vicariously.

We sat in silence for a time, and it occurred to me we were attending a silent worship service. Perhaps we were.

Tim pulled out his bottle and insisted I drink another bit with him. And then after a somewhat extended period of sipping and reflecting, the bottles were empty and the sun was sinking toward the tree tops once again. Tim started the engine and in a few minutes we were back at the shack, where I promptly said to Dottie, who had returned from her shopping trip, "I Ttink I'll just go to bed. I'm not really hungry." Tim told Dottie we had been on a sight seeing tour, which was the truth, and he then beat a hasty retreat. What a guy!

FRIENDS(29)
Lifelong Bonds

During a long life I have made friends every where I lived or traveled and in no way do I want to diminish the value of any of those friendships. I have chosen here to comment briefly on five whose memory I cherish.

Ken Vanden Berg, Bob Van Dyk, Bill Jesiek, Bill Van Oss and Bill Orr have all played significant roles in my life at different times. All have died except Bill Jesiek, and I communicate with him often by phone or e-mail.

Ken Vanden Berg was my childhood pal and we were inseparable for the first twelve years of our lives. Ken was a school athlete; I was not, but we managed to find enough time to do all the things that boyhood required, many of which I have related in *My Paradise; Dad's Hell* such as "The Great Black Lake Sea Battle" and our apple thrower accomplishments. In my memory, as we meander our way home from school, I still sit with him under the culvert at the bottom of Oosting's Hill where Lugers Road crosses Cook's Creek turning over rocks to catch the crayfish that lurked there and head for home dripping wet.

We were Boy Scouts and hunters. We reveled in the suppers put on by the Ladies Aid Society at the church and were fascinated by the older men who ate their entire dinners, including peas, from their knives and always asked for seconds. We compared notes on the merits of the family automobiles differing on which was the better.

Ken's mother Cornelia often had a piece of unfrosted chocolate cake for us we arrived at the Vanden Berg house after school. Father Henry drove his truck to take us to the place where we were to pitch our tent for a week as a scouting adventure, and drove with us in the back of the truck to the annual church picnic at Allegan State Park.

It was the Vanden Bergs who took in our whole family for a week when our house burned down on a Saturday in March 1933, the coldest day ever recorded in Holland. I was thirteen. Our arrival made nine in a house with only two bedrooms. It was the very worst part of the depression, the weekend that President Roosevelt closed all the banks. The next morning after each of the nine of us had made the necessary trip to the outside privy and after a long prayer of thanks by Henry for God's goodness, we were fed from their limited larder, which called for a breakfast of fat pork, white bread and black coffee before going to church. The fat pork was just that; there was no lean. I had never drunk coffee before. We gave thanks to the Lord several times that morning for his beneficences.

Ken and I became step brothers when, a short time after the death of his mother and my father the two survivors were married. Twenty five years later we celebrated their silver wedding anniversary on the deck of our house on the north side of the lake.

Bob Van Dyk was the minister's son, so the three of us were friends from the beginning. At the two room school to which we walked each morning, Bob and I were in the same grade; Ken, a few months younger, was a grade behind us. We all played marbles "for keeps," played baseball and teased the girls at recess. Bob could not participate in all of our activities as he went home in an entirely different direction, but as our grade school years came to an end, he was in command of one boat in our fleet during the Great Black Lake Sea Battle.

When his father came to school to teach catechism (imagine that in a public school!) Bob went into hiding after the lesson while the rest of us waited for the minister to say his adieus to the teacher before leaving in his ancient Model T Ford. When Reverend Van Dyk was seated in his flivver and started the engine, a covey of us would appear, hoist the back end of his vehicle off the ground until he pushed the pedal to go forward. In a few seconds when his wheels were spinning at a great rate, we dropped him and with a screech of burning rubber he went off to pursue his other ministerial functions.

During our high school years Bob lettered in football, Ken lettered in basketball and I enjoyed hunting and fishing.

On graduation from Hope College, Bob went to dental school, Ken went to medical school and I went into the navy. We saw each other only occasionally for many years, but maintained our friendships.

When Dottie and I were planning our adventure in Canada to attend the Rotary convention at Calgary, Dottie and I phoned Bob, who was retired and living in the Seattle area. We arranged to have dinner following our return from Calgary before our flight east. We met at the famous sky needle restaurant for a wonderful dinner and learned that he had uncontrollable diabetes. He died a few months later. As I was writing this, a decade after Bob's death, his widow, Linda, called while visiting a daughter in Orlando.

Bill Jesiek entered my life in a Model "A" Ford coupe with a rumble seat. The senior Jesiek brothers, Bill's father Otto and his brother operated a boat livery and small boat building shop just inside the shipping channel to Lake Michigan at the west end of Black Lake, which a short time later was renamed Lake Macatawa. Bill was a couple of years older than I, and thus allowed to drive his car to school. There were no buses, so all of us "country kids" either hitched a ride, as in my case, or rode with a parent or neighbor who worked in town. Bill responded one day to my thumb request, and as he had another passenger, I was assigned to the rumble seat, a great experience.

Our friendship continued to grow over the years, and although my years in the navy and other activities frequently interrupted our adventures together, we have kept in touch and shared our life experience vicariously. When Dottie and I were to be married I invited Bill to be my best man and he and his wife, Ginny, drove over from their retirement home on the west coast of Florida to be present. We have had a number of visits since, but now that none of us can drive, we visit solely by e- mail.

I met Bill Van Oss when I was a junior at Hope College and he arrived as a freshman from Burnip's Corners. He was a huge man with a ready grin and innumerable stories that reflected either his boyhood and youth on his father's dairy farm, or were inherited from a foot loose grandfather who, as a boy had ventured to South America and the Orient working his passage on tramp steamers.

Bill received an appointment to the naval academy, adding to my frustration at not getting one, but nevertheless our friendship continued to grow as we rose through the ranks of naval officers. As I was wrestling with the idea of resigning my regular navy commission and accepting one in the reserve, Bill spent a good deal of time with us and was of good counsel.

At the time of his retirement I had been on active duty for training at the Naval War College, and Bill was on the staff of the Naval Reserve Officers Training Corps at Cornel University, He honored me by requesting that I read his orders at the time of his retirement.

On a last visit with Bill and his wife Nola at their home overlooking the San Francisco International Airport, we learned of his impending death, which occurred within weeks of our visit.

Bill Orr was different. Our friendship did not develop easily, but eventually we became very close, partially through the aid of his wife, another Ginny. When we returned to Holland after my naval service, it was our intent to develop our twenty-five acre parcel of wooded land on a bay of the lake. The only access to our property was a short graveled road that extended a few hundred feet from where the Orr house stood and ended abruptly at our property line.

Bill resented our presence and vigorously talked against our development until we were well into the process when he realized he could do nothing to prevent it. We won his friendship originally by inviting him to keep his newly acquired thirty-two foot sloop at the dock we had built around the pilings set by

Clarence Owen using for the decking the tailings from the oak we cut for flooring in our new house.

It was Bill who livened up our parties with his quips and yarns. His vast array of tools often came to our rescue in time of need, and his wife endeared herself to us with an occasional gift of home made bread and, at Christmas time with a box of her wonderful fudge.

Years later, when we had moved to Florida, Bill and Ginny were given the privilege of occupying the winter residence of a Holland manufacturer near Vero Beach for a month each year in exchange for Bill using his skills to maintain and improve the property. It was there that we spent some time together each winter until ultimately he died of testicular cancer. His farewell quip was, "I'll write if I find work wherever I'm going."

Bill James claimed to his dying day that it was gunfire from the U.S.S. Monssen controlled by me that wounded him on D-day during the capture of Saipan in the Marianna Islands. We actually met in 1952 when we both were instructors at the University of Minnesota Naval Reserve Officers Training Corps unit teaching students there in the various courses presented by our department.

The James visited us early on in Michigan as they were en route to Taiwan for duty at the United States Embassy, one of his last assignments prior to retirement. For all the years afterward we were in close touch with each other, and had family visits every few years. After retirement from the United States Marine Corps, Bill worked for the Southern Railway amd we visited as we drove back and forth to Florida.

In retirement Billl and Peggy lived in a beautiful condo in Vero Beach and we frequently spent weekends together. Our last extensive time together was when we took a two week cruise to Alaska. When Bill died it was I who delivered his eulogy at a private service sponsored by the Marine Corps League in Vero. My voice cracked as I spoke of our long and very close friendship.

CHAPTER (30)
NEWS FROM THE PAST
"From Days Gone By"

Some of the best reading in the valley is contained in the columns of "The Fulton County News," a weekly that publishes whatever is available to publish. Its pages are filled with local news submitted by its correspondents in all the communities in the county, some only cross roads identified with names like Coalton, Coalville and Coaldale. The correspondents are mostly women paid a pittance by the inch for news of their communities, generally ordinary events in the lives of ordinary people doing the ordinary things that hold communities together and make the nation strong. I was living through the Fulton county weekly, the old gag mimicking "The New York Times'" mast head statement, "All the news that's fit to print" as modifiedtobe, "All the new that fits, we print." fits, we print."

The Fulton County News

417 E. Market Street, McConnellsburg, PA

A County Seat Weekly Newspaper

Periodicals Postage Paid at McConnellsburg, Pennsylvania 17233

U.S. PUBLICATION NO. 211820

Subscription Rates: $21 year in county; $22 out-of-county; $26 out-of-state

Postmaster: Send address changes to:
Fulton County News, P.O. Box 635, McConnellsburg, PA 17233
PHONE 485-3811 or 4513 Fax: 485-5187

The paper is fleshed out with stories on local high school sports, a few items of state interest, a smattering of national and international news, legal ads, classified and display advertising, and so forth, but the most interesting columns are those with items from issues published as much as ninety years ago, titled "From Days Gone By." The content is similar to the community reports submitted by the present day correspondents, but reflects the tenor of the earlier times.

With dates and quotation marks purposely omitted, but most items reproduced in their entirety except where indicated, here are a few selections:

The Clouser place, known as the Olde Stone Inn, was the scene of a disgraceful occurrence on Saturday night when more than 40 persons from Orbisonia and Mount Union staged free-for-all riot.....

Twenty of the more than 40 persons involved in the free-for-all at Clouser's Inn last Saturday night are being held under bond for court. Squire L.H. Wible conducted the hearing on Friday afternoon in the courtroom, which was filled to capacity. One Huntingdon attorney said, "Probably nothing like such a crowd was ever before involved in a hearing before a justice of the peace in central Pennsylvania."

An Essex car in which Fred Charlton and Ralph Waugh were riding crashed into a tree along the National Pike last week. Both boys were rendered unconscious, but were not badly hurt – considering the condition of the car.

Mrs. Leon Stevens of Fort Littleton has been quite poorly.

Burton A. Winter, who has lived in Kansas for he last 53 years writes that this has been one of the hottest and driest summers that state has ever had. They just experienced thirty successive days when the temperature was over 106. Mr. Winter says, I wished many times I were back in Pennsylvania to live and die."

Clyde Barton Plessinger and Doris Schmitthenner were married September 2.

Mrs. Rudolph Snyder of Knobsville had the misfortune to fall and break her ankle.

Mr. and Mrs. Horace Peck, who live in Thomastown, were troubled with a nest of yellow jackets in their home, so they got out their vacuum cleaner and exterminated thousands of the pests.

While many barns in Western Pennsylvania carried this message, we looked far and wide until we found this one in good readable condition. When I stepped out of the car to take this photo, a woman appeared and demanded that I get off her property.

Emory W. McClain of New Grenada bought a new Chevrolet.

Harry Grissinger, Jr., went to Wade Brady's farm at Big Cove Tannery on Tuesday to buy a bull, accompanied by Claude Souders and Willis Seville. The four men tried to load the bull on the truck, when it suddenly bolted, tearing the ring from its nose, throwing Souders against a fence post and giving chase to Seville. Seville managed to get inside the truck as the bull made another lap around it, finally jumping up on the hood and getting caught between the bumper and the radiator. At this point, Souders jumped on the bull and held its head until Seville stepped out of the truck and handed him a pocket knife with which he cut the bull's throat. Souders received minor injuries.

Fred Heckman and Harry Heisel of Wells Tannery have gone to Buckhorn to dig coal.

Mr. and Mrs. Earl Strait of Harrisonville celebrated their 25th wedding anniversary two weeks ago and are celebrating again, having learned this week that they had won a brand new 1966 Pontiac Catalina. Mr. Strait's name was on the winning ticket drawn at the chicken barbecue sponsored by the Blue Ridge Summit Sportsmen's Club on Saturday night.

Leo Golden of Mays Chapel took a truck load of peaches to Hopewell on Friday.

Sheriff Mellott has sold the meat market he started a year ago to Harvey Raker. The latter will retain H. E. Brown, the present manager, in that capacity. Mr. Raker is also a school teacher and conducts a milk route that supplies McConnelsburg.

The corn crop this year will be no ways near normal.

The untimely death of Mrs. Estella O. Mellott of Needmore forced the cancellation of plans for a party at the local American Legion hall to be given in her honor by her fellow union workers at Sagner, Inc. Mrs. Mellott was the first employee....to retire and collect benefits from the union's retirement plan.

Lester Mann of Mays Chapel has gone to a six-years logging job above Cumberland.

The northwest corner of the tower of the local Methodist Church had some stones broken from it on Monday evening when Ben McLucas lost control of his new motor truck while rounding the square, ran up over the curb and hit the church.

A cat and her kittens were all killed on Wednesday when lightning struck the home of Mrs. Mary Mort at Clear Ridge.

Rev. H. L. Jarrett is sporting a new 1927 Chevrolet Landeau. That's what comes of being the "marrying parson" of Fulton County.

A cow owned by Ross L. Mellott of Sipes Mill gave birth to triplets last week. The same cow had twin calves a year ago.

John Chamberlain of Wells Tannery accidentally shot himself last Wednesday with a high powered rifle, the bullet crushing the middle toe of the left foot so badly that Dr. Sipes of Everett had to amputate the toe.

Ernest Sprowl of Wells Tannery, who broke his leg while playing ball four weeks ago, is now exercising with two wooden helpers.

Cecil Lynch of Mays Chapel is not going to starve this winter. He canned 82 quarts of peaches this last week.

Wlliam Grissinger has returned from Harrisburg, where he visited his nieces. Mr. Grissinger rode a horse in the McConnellsburg Centennial parade 50 years ago, but rode in an automobile in the sesquicentennial parade a couple of weeks ago.

The Fulton county commissioners approved the purchase of the S. W. Kirk house ...for use as a courthouse annex. (Samuel Wesley Kirk was Dottie's great uncle.)

A daring daylight robbery took place at the Glen Nell cafeteria early Wednesday morning about 7:00 a.m. when a customer threw a cup of hot coffee in the face of the waitress, Mrs. Gladys Seville, scooped up the contents of the cash register and fled south toward the schoolhouse in an old model car.

Bonnie, the seven-year-old son of Ira Mellott of Knobsville, was bitten on the foot by a cooperhead snake last Saturday. His leg swelled clear to the hip, but the swelling is reducing at this time.

Elmer Bennett, an elderly resident of Artemas was scalded all over the front of his body last week when the crown seat of his old steam engine blew out, causing the boiler door to open unexpectedly.

***** *****

The following are excerpts from recent "Correspondents' Notes" in The News:

Tim and John McGarvey attended the Orioles vs. Yankees baseball game on Saturday.

The weekend weather was very pleasant after a very hot spell last week.

Marge Chamberlain would like to express her appreciation to everyone who aided her husband, John, after he fell on the street across from MacDonald's Pharmacy on Thursday. A little girl went into the drug store for help, and a man who came along, stopped his car to help John get up from the street....May God bless all the folks who were so helpful.

The annual Sherman's Valley Church of the Brethren pig roast supper was held at 5:00 p.m. last evening at the Dodson picnic area....There was a fine attendance, and John and I attended this annual event, too.....some of the musicians were Jackie Kriner, Vicki Miller, Darrell and Clair Dodson, Pastor Riley and Jerry Gant.

Charlie and Mary Cutshall would like to thank all their good neighbors for he fine food, visits and prayers recently.

Olive McQuait, Lyn Logan of Texas, Brian and Emily Ramsey and Chad Ramsey had dinner with Roger and Pat Ramsey on Monday evening. Adding to the evening were granddogs Dakota and Chase, who enjoyed romping with Sasha.

We are happy to have Dorothy (Kirk) Bertsch and husband Fritz enjoy some time down the valley at Kirk's Bottom. They are Florida residents in other months.

***** *****

Wouldn't it be great if all the news were like this, rather than the constant drumbeat of reports about a world in uproar? Most of the national and international news seems irrelevant to the people iof the mountains and the valleys of central Pennsylvania.

DECISION (31)
A Painful Departure

For five years when we not off adventuring either in Wells Tannery or elsewhere, we enjoyed living in our beautiful three bedroom two bath house in Country Club Cove, a part of Miles Grant. We particularly enjoyed the open lanai, the adjoining kitchen and a yard filled with flowering bushes and fruit trees overlooking a slowly flowing creek.

Our orange tree produced great quantities of Honey Bells, the sweetest and most delicious oranges in the world. We became experts using the fruit picker that had come with the house to pluck the oranges above our reach either from the ground or from the top of our seven foot ladder. The grapefruit tree was even more prolific and the fruit almost equally sweet. We gave away bushels of fruit and sent holiday packages to our families. Our third citrus tree was grafted to produce both lemons and limes, but it was too close to the house and required frequent pruning, even more than the orange and grapefruit trees.

We entertained frequently, usually serving a dinner from the back yard barbeque or one of my famous meals of rice and curry with a half dozen or more condiments to complete the entrée.

All these things and more about our living conditions were most enjoyable, but there were other elements involved. My weakened back made it difficult or impossible to do the yard work. We did have a capable young man who came once a week for a half day, but he couldn't keep up with all the mowing and pruning that the place required.

By the spring of 2003 I had come to the conclusion that we personally needed to live in a more supportive atmosphere due to the fact that over time we would become physically weaker as the years passed. We had investigated our options and settled on Sandhill Cove, a continuing care retirement community located across the north fork of the St. Lucie River from Stuart as the place to be. Dottie was not so sure, but at my insistence agreed to the move.

We talked to our children and grandchildren to inform them of our decisions. I wrote an e-mail in the spring of 2003 that summarizes our situation at that time and the decision we had made. I addressed it to my four children, and three of my four grandchildren assuming that Buck and Cindy would inform their family.

"We have decided that the time has come when we can no longer maintain a single family home, and for this and other reasons we have decided to move into a continuing care retirement community on the St. Lucie River in Palm City called Sandhill Cove. It is across the river from Stuart. This is still in Martin County.

"Some of you know we have been considering this for some time. We have been very deliberate in preparing to make this decision. We have visited Sandhill Cove many times; attended a number of seminars or luncheons there, talked to friends who live there, and so forth.

"The timing of our decision of our decision has occurred because the specific type of apartment we want became available. It is a two-bedroom, two-bath apartment with a well-equipped kitchen, a fairly large living room-dining room, a "Florida Room" and patio, all on the first floor.

"We do not close on the apartment until we return from Wells Tannery in the fall, about the first of October. We have made the necessary deposit and are making arrangements to finalize on our return. This timing, agreed to by the management is intended, among other things, to give us time to sell our house.

"There are many things we would like to tell you about all of this, but here are a few:

(1) This an up-scale establishment with numerous amenities and activities;

(2) We receive one meal per day (more if we wish to pay for them);

(3) Weekly cleaning and flat laundry service;

(4) In-house nursing serve as required – an extra charge if extensive;

(5) A nursing home and assisted living facility is also on the grounds and a part of the program;

(6) There are guest rooms available for a nominal charge – continental breakfast included; (We add this comment since our second bedroom is destined to become a combination office, den and computer facility);

(7) There is a well-equipped wood shop for me!!

"Much more detail is available at their website, www.sandhilcove.com. This site is not too good at present, but scheduled for upgrade. At present we're busy getting the necessary physical exams, filling out required forms and making plans for our trek up north in a few days.

"It would be nice if we could have some help during our move and the preparation for it. As that will be in the fall, you all can talk about it and plan for what can be done to help us. There is time.

"Looking to the time of our move, we will have a surplus of many things, unless it all goes with the house: a complete set of bedroom furniture, plus other household items, small tables, patio chairs, etc., some linens and garage stuff. Any of you who want any or all of this may have it if you can transport it. Just don't fight about it - - it ain't worth it.

"This is probably a big enough dose for one morning. Love to all, DAD/ GRANDPA."

When all of the preliminaries for our move were complete, we started our annual trek to the shack stopping along the way for family visits. It was a long drive from our last visits in North Carolina and we were tired when we completed the treacherous descent from the mountain into the valley and crossed the wooden bridge into the meadow. Ron had done his part in preparing the place for our arrival by turning on the water, starting the furnace and plugging in the refrigerator, while Charlene Dodson, our regular cleaning lady, worked her magic by making the place entirely presentable, including the washing and stretching of the old curtains and clearing out the multitude of lady bugs that swarm to the shack for shelter during the cold months each year.

SANDHILL COVE (32)
A Final Move

Upon arrival at Sandhill Cove to take up residence in our new apartment, we parked our car and waited a few minutes until the arrival of the moving van with its three movers followed by Buck and Susan in their rental car. It was after two in the afternoon and the clock was running.. One of the movers remarked as he descended from the cab, "We ain't never gonna git that stuff moved in today, We'll have to come back tamarra. If we stay you'll have to pay time and a half,"

My retort was, "You are going to move it all in today. The estimator said it would be one load on one truck accompanied by three men and that the move would be completed in one day. He gave us a flat price. I have the contract to prove it. You were an hour late getting started, so you may be an hour late getting finished." Although they were a bit sullen, the movers went to work.

Buck and Susan joined the movers to speed things up a little and gave directions for placement of things in accordance with the chart we had prepared. Dottie and I tried to move a few light things, but Buck said, rather abruptly, "You two are going to be in the way. Go over to the library, and don't come back. We'll get you when we're finished."

Four hours later Susan came and gave us permission to return to our apartment. Every piece of furniture, with one exception was in its place in accordance with the drawing we had made. Somehow we had misread a dimension and the beautiful five foot circular glass top would not fit on the dining room table as planned. If placed on the table there would be nowhere for the diners to sit. Finally, some weeks later, after trying to give the beautiful piece of plate glass to various charities, we obtained permission to give it to a Sandhill Cove employee, an exception to a policy of our new community.

The movers' feelings were somewhat assuaged when I slipped them each a ten dollar bill and remarked, "Don't spend it all in one place, or at least drive carefully." After our many expressions of appreciation for their efforts we sent Buck and Cindy off to their motel and collapsed into bed for a good night's sleep in our new home.

Soon after we were settled in, I checked out the woodworking shop dubbed "Sawdust and Gomorah," and concluded that a considerable portion of my time would be spent there. My first and as it turned out, my only, project was to build nesting houses for the species of birds I had been interested since boyhood. This project took many months including the time I spent scavenging for lumber around the Sandhill Cove property. I enlisted the help of employees in the maintenance and housekeeping groups who would let me know when equipment or supplies arrived encased in wooden boxes or carried on pallets that were to be discarded. I spent much time dismantling the boxes and pallets and gluing the recovered wood with waterproof glue to provide the materials for my project.

After many months of salvaging and reworking the materials into usable lumber, I had produced enough finished parts to make six wood duck nesting boxes and six each of bluebird and wren houses. I loaded them all in the large trunk of our Cadillac in anticipation of our trip north to Wells Tannery

One of the many things we brought to Sandhill Cove was the aging bicycle upon which I had ridden around the golf course at Miles Grant for all the years we were residents there either in Hanson's Landing or, after marriage, in Country Club Cove. From our new residence I rode for miles every day on roads and sidewalks both inside and outside of the community as a leg exercise in lieu of the walking that had become unbearably painful. I couldn't walk, but I could ride the bike without pain.

In early May of two thousand seven during my regular morning ride, there was a sudden rattling under me, the bike fell out from under me and I skidded on my backside for a few feet after falling. I discovered that all the spokes in the rear wheel had broken and were hanging from the hub of the wheel. It was a Sunday and I went home to peruse the classified ads with more than usual concentration, starting with the section titled "Merchandise under $50.00."

I began calling the numbers in the ads mentioning bicycles, only to find that the bikes for sale were for children, were of unsuitable size, were located fifty or more miles away or had already been sold. My last call was to a Port St. Lucie number, and the man said, "The bike's been sold, but you are welcome to come and take a look. I have others." That was a motivating invitation. I was thinking bicycle when I should have been thinking about the bird houses and wood duck boxes that occupied virtually every cubic inch of the trunk of the car.

After much searching down one way streets and blind street endings, I finally found the place with the bicycles. The owner and his wife came out to the driveway forthwith, the owner saying as he approached me, "The bike you saw advertised didn't please the lady who came to look, so it's still for sale. Take a look." The bike was a beauty, more resplendent than any I had every owned, and I handed the man a ten dollar bill which he promptly handed to his wife for safekeeping. "I'll help you load it into the trunk," he said. It was only then upon opening the trunk that we discovered the unassembled bird houses and duck boxes that filled virtually every inch of space. I had not been feeling well for more than a week but I was determined to get that bike home. Further, I didn't want to make another trip to get it, so we disassembled it and with much maneuvering managed to get the frame into the back seat of my car and tossed the wheels in on top of the load.

When I got home a new neighbor helped me unload my new acquisition and the next day I set out to assemble the new bike. By the time I had finished in the middle of the afternoon, my malaise had increased enough that I felt I should call our doctor to see if he could see me. "Dr. Gaeta has patients scheduled for well into the evening hours," said the recipient of my call, and handed the phone to the doctor's assistant, a male nurse practitioner. "Your best bet is to go to the emergency room at either of the hospitals," and then he added, "At this time of the day you are best off going to Martin South as the roads to and from the main hospital will be crowded. At the time it was given that counsel was the logical thing to do, but not long after it proved to be a big mistake.

I drove the ten miles or so to the hospital, parked the car in one of the spaces marked for the emergency room and put the car keys over the driver's visor, as was my wont. I walked into the emergency room and registered, after which the attendant said, "Take a seat. Your wait will be at least an hour." I sat down, but in a few minutes my name was called. The attendant needed some more information. I rose from my chair and all the lights in the universe formed a kaleidoscope before my eyes as I slumped to the floor.

The next thing I knew was the howling of the siren of the ambulance in which I was riding en route to the newly established cardiac unit at Martin Memorial Hospital. I was quickly established in a cardiac intensive care room and fitted with numerous breathing equipments, intravenous tubes and other paraphernalia with a private duty nurse installed at my bedside.

Dr. Danchenko, who became my cardiologist and Dr. Gaeta, our internist called an incredulous Dottie to inform her of my situation and advise her that I would no doubt require open heart surgery. With that Dottie picked up the phone and started calling family. Daughter Mary Jo, herself a cardiologist practicing in tidewater North Carolina, responded that she would be at my bedside by morning. The next morning Dottie called Mary Sommer, director of assisted living at Sandhill Cove, to tell her.

By the time Dottie got to the hospital the next morning, Mary Jo was there, had already consulted with the physicians and learned that I would require a triple by pass and mitral valve repair. The rest of the family arrived and spoke individually to me. With an exception or two about which I was told only after my recovery, I "out of it" for several days, and only tried to alter my situation with some hardly credible requests to take some drastic actions in my brokerage account. It had been twenty-four hours since I ha+d had anything to eat or drink. My mouth was parched and I demanded water, but only received an occasional ice chip; I was being hydrated by intravenous drip in anticipation of surgery.

On the day I was scheduled for my surgery the open heart surgical team had been operating since early morning and had performed two lengthy procedures prior to mine. In the middle of the afternoon, after consulting with the assembled family, it was jointly decided that I should be stabilized and surgery scheduled for early the next day. I lay on the gurney, not aware of any of this, when the surgeon and anesthesiologist, both wearing scrub suits and surgical masks came to apprise me of that decision. Dr. Cook, the surgeon, not mentioning that the decision to delay surgery had already been made, asked me if it was all right to delay. I nodded in the affirmative.

I t was then the turn of the anesthesiologist, who peered over the top of his mask with eyes that appeared to me to be oriental. He introduced himself, "I'm Dr. el Ushi, your anesthesiologist," and then the bootless question, "Is it OK with you to delay the surgery? We're all very tired." I nodded in agreement and managed to say, "Go home and get plenty of rest so you can take care of me in the morning," and then, because his name sounded Japanese to me, I added, "But don't go right home; stop at that Japanese restaurant on East Ocean and get some sushi."

He said, "What the hell is sushi?"

I said, incredulously, "You're Japanese and don't know what sushi is? It's practically the Japanese national dish."

"I'm not Japanese, I'm Egyptian, and I never heard of sushi." We had a good laugh and I lapsed into sleep. I was not conscious of anything until early afternoon the next day when the doctors aroused me and told me the procedures had been long, but successful. I complained that the inside of my left thigh hurt a bit, but otherwise I felt no pain. Dr. Cook explained that they had removed a blood vessel from my leg for use as a by-pass of the affected area.

Our minister, Reverend Jim Bailey had visited as soon as he heard I was hospitalized, and his visits continued during my hospital stay The family visited two at a time and during Buck's visit I told him about the Cadillac left in the emergency room parking lot at Martin South and asked that he and grandson, Skipper, drive down and pick it up. "The keys are over the visor, and the trunk is full of bird houses and duck boxes all ready to be assembled."

A day or so later, Dr. Cook advised us that he was pleased with my condition, that I would remain in intensive care for another three days, followed by about ten days of extended care and rehabilitation, after which I would go to Sandhill Cove's Water's Edge, our community's extended care facility. The ten days of extended care passed with the tender care of the assigned nurses, who kept me properly medicated, fed and disentangled from all the equipment serving to keep me on the mend. Except for the relatively mild problem with the wounds on my leg, I suffered no pain as a result of the operations. What I did experience was the pain caused by the inoperable preexisting stenosis and other damage to my lower back

After another ambulance ride I arrived at Water's Edge, the continuing care facility on the grounds of Sandhill Cove and assigned to a room overlooking the ponds lying between me and some of the villas It was June sixth. I was very weak, but with the help and guidance of two dedicated certified nursing assistants I set about over time learning to walk, to go to the bath room, to shower and otherwise care for myself. Dottie came every day, did my laundry several times a week, carrying the soiled clothes one way to our apartment and the clean clothes the other. She was becoming exhausted as I was gaining in strength.

After a few days Dottie began to come for dinner, having it delivered to my room from the main kitchen, one of the services provided by Sandhill Cove. Not so Dottie's pre-dinner cocktail; she ordered it at the lounge in the main building and carried it over with her dinner, a distance of a couple hundred feet. This went on for several evenings until the food and beverage manager spotted her carrying the cocktail glass away from the bar area. "Against the rules," proclaimed the manager, "All glass must remain in the lounge."

Resourceful Dottie turned to the bar tender and said, "Pour this into a plastic cup, add some ice and another shot of vodka." With that she made her usual departure from the lounge and we enjoyed another meal together in my room.

There were communication glitches as I became stronger and more demanding; sometimes ornery. There were several residents who walked in the morning on the cart path not far outside my window and waved greetings or walked over to my window to give me a cheerful greeting. Flowers, candy and plants arrived. The secretary of the Rotary club arrived with a prize I had won in a fund raising lottery for which I had bought tickets many months earlier. The contents of the package? Chanel number five perfume, toilet water and bath powder plus a tube of hand lotion and a dainty handkerchief. I happily and appreciatively consigned these to a deserving Dottie.

As I began to feel better I also felt a need to communicate more broadly, but the phone in my room had been altered to make it available only for local calls. I discovered that a Sprint calling card would enable me to make long distance calls. A helpful certified nursing assistant (CNA) undertook to buy one for me and then I had telephone access to the entire world..

My impression was that I was recovering well and doing, all the things I was told to do, including some exercises with the assistance of a CNA, but somehow the hierarchy at Waters Edge and Mary Sommer thought differently and expressed their concerns to Dottie who in turn passed them on to me. I set out to demonstrate to her all the things I was doing for myself, but admittedly I couldn't walk any more than the few steps to the bathroom.

Physical therapy began and I was walked up and down the hall several times with assistance and performed the various prescribed exercises under supervision. After only a few such sessions, the physical therapist told me I was having the last supervised physical therapy. I objected strenuously but was told that Medicare rules would not allow any more paid therapy. I said I would pay for additional sessions myself, and would have done so but within a day the therapist had discovered a way under which my care would be paid by Medicare.

There were appointments with Doctors Danchenko, Cook and Gaeta for checkups to which appointments I was transported by ambulance. Each proclaimed, "You are doing just fine."

Eventually the great day came when I was delivered to our home for a pre-release check during which I moved about the apartment using a walker. Several adjustments were made to accommodate to my needs. Some furniture was moved slightly, our throw rugs and living room runners were removed and a removable seat with rails was installed in my bathroom.

The following day I returned home for good; a happy day!

But there were still hurdles. Physical therapy, now in the apartment began anew. A follow up visit with Dr. Danchenko revealed no change in my accelerated heart beat. He noted that eventually, if the rate didn't lower we should consider cardio version. Several months later another check revealed there was no change. My heart was being overburdened by its rapid beat. The cardiologist said, "You really should consider cardio version. If it works, it can prolong your life."

I leaped at the idea. "When can it be done?" It was Tuesday, and the doctor indicated the procedure could be scheduled for any Thursday in the future. I leaped at the opportunity and asked, "How about the day after tomorrow?"

The doctor said, "Fine, I'll set it up." During the intervening day and during preparation for the procedure, many people, mostly lacking in knowledge told me how dangerous and painful the whole thing would be. After a couple of hours of wiring and rewiring me as I lay on the gurney it was rolled into the operating room, where I lay with some apprehension awaiting the arrival of Dr. Danchenko. When he arrived I received a mild anesthetic and after a few minutes I asked when the procedure would begin. "It's over," said the doctor. "You can go home in an hour."

My blood pressure and heart rate dropped to normal and have stayed that way. I take my vital signs every Wednesday and report them to the doctor at each six-month appointment. On the first of these visits following my cardio version the cardiologist said I was as normal as a person in his eighties can be. I wept a bit with joy. There are occasional changes in my medications, most often a reduction.

Our exercise routines have returned to normal. I rise ten or fifteen minutes before six, perform my bathroom chores and then do twenty minutes of stretching exercises. It is then off to the weight room where I spend twenty minutes pedaling the stationary bike and watching the morning news. The next step is into the swimming pool, where I walk twenty lengths of the pool at the four foot depth while Dottie swims the same lengths. I then spend ten minutes in the spa, where the one hundred three degree heat and massaging streams give considerable relief to my back. Then, if the sky is not cloudy, I spend twenty minutes in the morning sun on my back and then the reverse, a preventative against the return of my eczema.

Life is good here. Neither of us is allowed to drive any great distance, although we do manage to drive to a nearby restaurant; it's a nice change from our routine and the short trip is sufficient to keep the battery charged. Transportation to professional offices is provided by limousine at no extra charge.

Our regular meals in the main dining room are more varied and better prepared than those at any restaurant.

Sometimes we eat with other residents, but often alone by choice following a cocktail, either at home or in the lounge. We attend the weekly movie when we feel like it, attend the monthly informational meetings led by the executive director and occasionally enjoy the weekly travelogue. Once a month our forum committee sponsors a presentation by an outstanding citizen, most often a professional from the Treasure Coast area.

Although we have not participated because of time constraints, every day is bridge day at Sandhill Cove; everything from beginners' sessions to duplicate. Wednesdays we have a table or two of poker and I am a happy participant. As I write we are planning to take a cruise in company with a group of other residents. Our lives are the best they can be as we go through our nineties.

I try to write a page or two of my memoirs every day, but am often delinquent. My goal is to have them all published before my death. Occasionally I receive a letter, card or e-mail reminding me of an incident in which I participated long ago. A year or so ago one such reminder came from the present football coach at my alma mater requesting former Hope College football players to submit accounts of their performances on the gridiron. I accepted the challenge even though my participation had been extremely limited. Here is my account of an incident on the field in which I was a principal participant:

Field sports had not attracted me while I was in high school. I was far more interested in hunting, fishing, sailing and ice boating. Beside all that, I was too small, too young and too slow to be considered for any of the high school sports teams. College was different, I figured. I had beefed up to about a hundred and thirty pounds and had been hardened by my two year stint filling retorts at the local Heinz factory during pickle season.

I decided to go out for the freshman football team and find out what that sport was all about. Not knowing what else to do with a prospective candidate for the team who had never even seen a scholastic or any other football game, Coach Jack

Schouten, former athletic director, but now the freshman coach, assigned me to play guard. No doubt he felt that in this position I was least likely to spoil things by touching the football.

I played a few minutes in every game of our four game season that year (1937), Mostly I suffered cleat marks on my back in efforts to stop the opposing running backs. All this entitled me to an orange "1941" to be displayed on a dark blue sweater, for which I expended a few dollars from my pickle earnings.

When the fresh cucumber season was about over the next year, it was back to college and a stint with the varsity team. I must have been somewhat delusionary to think that at my now gross weight of a hundred forty pounds I could be anything but mincemeat on the gridiron.

However, I stuck it out and even played for a few minutes in game against Olivet, an opponent that was the doormat of the Michigan Intercollegiate Athletic Association at that time. The coach apparently trusted that I couldn't blow Hope's 35-0 lead in a single appearance. Our equipment in those depression years left much to be desired, and even so was in short supply due to budgetary restrictions. Today any team, collegiate or scholastic, would be laughed off the field should they appear in such dilapidated uniforms. Most of what we had was badly worn and repeatedly repaired.

Late in the season we played Hillsdale College, then the powerhouse of the conference, at our home field, Riverview Park down next to the Black River Swamp. It was the homecoming game for Hope, with our team facing a team that dominated the Michigan Intercollegiate Athletic Association. The quality of Hillsdale football in those days was such that they opened each season playing storied Notre Dame as a warm up for the big Catholic university.

We were doing well in this game against our powerful opponent going into the fourth quarter. As I recall it, the score was tied. Hope had the ball and had made several first downs, bringing the ball into Hillsdale territory. I, of course, was seated

*at the very end of the bench watching this great event with my
friend, Jim Hallen, who had also played a few minutes in the
Olivet game. That either of us might get to see action in this
game was hardly a possibility.*

*Suddenly Coach Hinga stood up and took a few steps
along the side line toward my end of the bench. "Bertsch," he
yelled, "Get over here right now." Had the coach gone nuts? Was
he going to send me into that meat grinder out there on the
field? He put his hand on my shoulder and said, "Bertsch, take
off your shoes," and then signaled the quarterback to call a time
out. My thought was, "What the hell is going on?"*

*The team trotted off the field and formed a circle around
the coach, the quarterback nd me. The players from the bench
formed a circle around us all. Addressing me, Coach Hinga said,
"Take off your pants." He didn't have to say anything to the
quarterback, who was already pulling off his pants, which were
ripped open from knee to thigh. In a trice the team was back on
the field. The quarterback was wearing my former pants and I
was holding my "new" pants together to hide my nakedness.*

*I'm pictured with the varsity football team in the 1939
Hope College yearbook, "The Milestone." I never earned a
varsity letter in football or any other sport, but perhaps it is
because I am pictured with the team in that yearbook or possibly
it is because there exists some other obscure record of my
football participation that I get letters from the coach every fall
informing me of the team's prowess and performance. Maybe I'll
get an honorary varsity "H" for my hundredth birthday in
recognition of the sacrifice of my pants so many years ago.*

There are many people around who have done great
things in their lifetimes and I give them their deserved
accolades. I also believe I have contributed fairly to the success
of my generation.

However, I am left with great concern for the future of the
United States. Our spending, both individually and as a nation
has been far greater than our savings and we are far over our

heads in debt to countries like China, India, Saudi Arabia and Indonesia. Our social programs, such as social security, Medicare and Medicaid, however idealistic they may be, are seriously under funded and over committed as we look the other way and dream that some fairy godmother is going to pay for our profligate spending. Our country is broke and it seems no one is trying to stabilize its future.

As a people we must learn to live in smaller houses, drive smaller and more efficient cars, save more of our earnings and insist that all levels of government operate on balanced budgets, while paying off the massive debt we have imposed on future generations. Only thus, combined with increased productivity, can the United States even dream of maintaining its position of influence in the world.

It is saddening to end the story of my life on such a depressing note, but we can hardly expect other countries to pay the debt that is being inherited by our children and several generations thereafter.

APPENDIX I
"A LOVE STORY IN 148 WORDS"

A few weeks before Valentine's Day one year the local newspaper conducted a contest in which entries with a Valentine theme were limited to one hundred fifty words or less. The winner would receive a small cash prize and other entries would be published..

I firmly believed that our love story was the most romantic and would win the prize if I could relate it in one hundred fifty words. I wrote and rewrote my entry a dozen times and finally whittled it down to one hundred forty-eight words. Here is what I submitted after many re-writes:

+A neighbor phoned, "Will you join us for bridge tonight?" She knew I was still grieving from the death of my beloved wife after years of Alzheimer's.

To "Who will be my partner?" I asked. She mentioned a widowed church parishioner I had met, but hardly knew. I accepted with reluctance.

On Valentine's Day the winning essay was published. It contained more than two hundred fifty words. Two others were published, each containing even more words.

APPENDIX II
Grandpa's Thoughts for a Happy Life

These are some notions or tenets that have been useful to me. They may prove to be useful to you. No claim is made for originality; almost none is original, and none is foolproof, but all are worth considering. This is a work in progress; kept it so!

1. Be content but never satisfied.
2. Money can't bring happiness, but it surely helps to make one comfortable until happiness comes along.
3. Do your best.
4. Some days it's better to be lucky rather than smart.
5. If you want to make an enemy, lend money to a friend or relative.
6. If you violate Item 5above (and there are times when it is appropriate) insist on a note signed by all recipients, an established interest rate, a prescribed mode and rate of payment and a date upon which the final payment is to be made.
7. If you give a gift, clearly identify it as such; don't expect repayment.
8. Remember "Look before you leap," but keep in mind that "He who hesitates is lost."
9. Shakespeare, summarizing item 8., wrote,
   "There is a tide in the affairs of men which taken at the flood leads on to fortune; missed all of life is spent in shallows and in misery...."
10. Do things throughout you life to improve the lot of your fellow man, both individually and collectively.
11. Maintain you belief in God, but don't claim him as yours exclusively; God is everywhere and in the life of each living person, whatever his religious association may be, if any.
12. Participate. Join a service club, a church, a hobby or interest group and/or a social organization.
13. Have one or more sedentary interests <u>and</u> several that involve physical activity.

14. Ben Franklin's "A penny saved is a penny earned," is applicable today, but it's more like "A thousand dollars saved is a thousand dollars earned," considering inflation.

15. Most geniuses are very expensive to maintain; for the most part it's better to be of average intelligence and do your best with of it.

16. Listen! You may find that others also have good ideas.

17. Don't get to believing you know all the answers. You don't.

18. Open your mind; think outside the box.

19. Read - - Keep a book or magazine in the bathroom just in case you get a few moments to read.

20. Have a place for everything and keep everything in its place - - well, almost everything. At least know where everything of importance in your life is.

21. If possible, delay at least overnight before making a major decision. Sleep has a way of clarifying and identifying the options and objectives.

22. Don't start vast projects with half vast ideas.

23. If you're going to go broke, go broke early in life while you still have a chance to recover.

24. Life isn't fair; get used to it.